Best Practices in Designing Courses with Open Educational Resources

Best Practices in Designing Courses with Open Educational Resources is a practical guide that assists faculty and institutions looking to adopt and implement open educational resources (OER) and to foster meaningful, effective learning experiences through the course design process. Chapters loaded with tips, case examples, and guidance from practitioners advise readers through each step necessary for sustainable OER initiatives, from preliminary planning and course redesign through teaching, learning, and faculty development.

Written by two authors with direct experience in training higher education professionals to use OER, this is a comprehensive resource for faculty, instructional designers, course developers, librarians, information technologists, and administrators hoping to rethink and refresh their curricula by moving beyond traditional textbooks. An authors' website expands the book with resources, templates, and examples of implementation models, including faculty development workshop OER materials that can be adopted by readers.

Olena Zhadko is Director of Online Education at Lehman College, City University of New York, USA. She has nearly 15 years of experience providing leadership in online education and innovative use of technology in teaching and learning.

Susan Ko is Faculty Development Consultant in the Office of Online Education and Clinical Professor in the History Department at Lehman College, City University of New York, USA. She is the author of *Teaching Online: A Practical Guide*, a leading book in the field of online teaching, and the series editor for the Best Practices in Online Teaching and Learning series. She has more than 20 years of online teaching and faculty development experience.

Best Practices in Online Teaching and Learning

Series Editor: Susan Ko

For a full list of titles in this series, please visit: www.routledge.com/Best-Practices-in-Online-Teaching-and-Learning/book-series/BPOTL

Best Practices in Designing Courses with Open Educational Resources

Olena Zhadko and Susan Ko

Routledge
Taylor & Francis Group

NEW YORK AND LONDON

First published 2020
by Routledge
52 Vanderbilt Avenue, New York, NY 10017

and by Routledge
2 Park Square, Milton Park, Abingdon, Oxon, OX14 4RN

*Routledge is an imprint of the Taylor & Francis Group, an
informa business*

Library of Congress Cataloging-in-Publication Data
A catalog record for this book has been requested

ISBN: 978-0-367-14069-4 (hbk)
ISBN: 978-0-367-14070-0 (pbk)
ISBN: 978-0-429-03001-7 (ebk)

Typeset in Bembo
by Apex CoVantage, LLC

Contents

Part I

Overview

Chapter 1

Introduction to OER
What's It All About?

Many of us have been teaching with open educational resources (OER) without even realizing it, while others have been intentional about OER use to support student learning. In fact, OER have been used to support learners for many years in higher education. Educators have traditionally pooled resources and shared course materials they have authored, well before the advent of the internet. Recently, with the increase in college tuition, OER have gained attention among higher education institutions as a possible solution to improve student retention and increase affordability by eliminating expensive textbooks or other commercially produced materials. The OER movement has not only resulted in millions of dollars saved by students but also in the improvement, redesign, and renewal of learning materials by faculty. Just as online education made us revisit instructional strategies, delivery methods, learning outcomes, and assessment measures, OER now serve as a catalyst to further innovation in education. In the competitive market in higher education, institutions also want to distinguish themselves as they create a path for student success. Institutions are striving to reduce time to graduation and increase student retention while providing quality learning experiences and preparing students for the job market. Colleges demonstrate their determination to remove barriers to student success by pursuing more affordable and accessible learning opportunities. Many colleges have launched different types of affordability initiatives. In many cases, the successful use of OER has been in the forefront of such initiatives. Additionally, there have been state, federal, or other funds available to institutions to promote and distribute OER.

Some of the benefits of using OER are obvious, like greater access and cost savings for students and possibly for institutions. Other benefits may be less apparent but may have even far more significant ramifications for education. For example, free textbooks and materials benefit students because they are more likely to be accessed. Also, OER can quickly disseminate the most current knowledge, whether in text or media. Furthermore, OER may allow materials to be remixed, shaped, and adapted by faculty to better fit course needs. Additionally, with OER, students have immediate access to course materials from the very beginning of the course. Finally, courses listed with the "zero-textbook cost" designation can empower students to make informed decisions about their course selection, potentially decreasing the time to degree attainment.

Defining Open

It is essential to define key terms and get familiar with the subtle or not so subtle differences. As defined by the Hewlett Foundation website, OER are "high-quality teaching, learning, and research materials that are free for people everywhere to use and repurpose" (n.d., para. 1).

The EDUCAUSE Learning Initiative (ELI, 2018 a, b, c) offers definitions of three related aspects of "open" initiatives—open educational content (OER), open educational practices, and open educational policies:

> Open educational resources (OER) are teaching, learning, and research materials in any medium that reside in the public domain or that have been released under an open license that permits no-cost access, use, adaptation, and redistribution by others. OER include textbooks, curricula, syllabi, lecture notes, video, audio, simulations, assessments, and any other content used in education. OER provide ubiquitous access to high-quality, effective learning materials that can be easily tailored and freely adapted, revised, expanded, translated, and shared with educators and learners around the world. OER support the practice of open education, an umbrella term for the mix of open content, practices, policies, and communities that, properly leveraged, can provide broad access to effective learning opportunities for everyone
>
> (ELI, OER Content, para. 1)

Open educational practices (OEP) are seen as a means for students and faculty to develop new approaches to co-creating knowledge, assessing student outcomes, and designing programs. . . . While educators often initially embrace open educational content as a way to maximize access to curricular materials and significantly reduce their costs, many instructors leverage OER to reconceptualize and improve pedagogy and advance authentic, participatory, engaged learning.

(ELI, OER Practices, para. 1)

Open education policies are formal regulations regarding support, funding, adoption, and use of open educational content and/or open education practices. Such policies can take many forms, including legislation from national, provincial, or state governments; institutional policies and guidelines; funder mandates; and declarations from influential bodies such as UNESCO.

(ELI, OER Policies, para. 1)

These key terms will help you navigate the world of OER and equip you with the necessary vocabulary. However, while you might be an avid OER adopter and/or creator, you don't necessarily have to become an OER policy maker—you can still benefit with open education policies in place, ensuring fewer barriers and more support systems to guarantee success. The fact that you engage in open educational practices does not necessarily mean that you only publish in open access journals, either.

The Cost of Free and/or Open

Another important definition to keep in mind is the difference between *free* and *open* when considering open educational resources. Learning materials found online and freely accessible do not necessarily equate to open. The licensing conditions will define the exact conditions for how materials can be used, and the fine print will specify the exact use cases and will help guide your OER adoption process.

OER are free (to students), but not all free materials are OER. Some people consider all content in the public domain as OER, even though it was not originally designed to be OER and has no explicit licensing setting forth the conditions of use. For example,

Jane Austen's novel *Pride and Prejudice* is in the public domain, but it is doubtful that Austen had intended it to be offered as OER.

While not all learning materials you will need for your class might be OER, you can leverage your library resources (for example, periodicals, ebooks, or other subscriptions) and other online content to provide essential course materials that are still free for students. We call these types of materials "free but not OER."

The term "zero-textbook cost," often used in conjunction with discussions about OER, means that students do not need to pay for learning materials.

But as noted by Young, "OER is not free, since it costs money to develop the materials, takes time for professors to evaluate and adopt them, and typically involves other campus-support services as well" (2018, para. 1). One study estimated the cost of building an OER course at an average of $11,700 (Griffiths et al., 2018). There have been several methodologies to estimate OER savings. For example, the OER Adoption Impact Calculator (https://impact.lumenlearning.com/) allows you to estimate the potential impact of OER in comparison with commercial texts (Wiley, 2018). There have been further studies that discuss sustainability models, support services, and additional costs to institutions to maintain and advance adoption and/or creation of OER course materials.

OER Initiatives

In an attempt to lower cost barriers to degree attainment, schools have moved beyond pilots of OER use to replacing expensive texts with OER and to developing full programs that are textbook free, called Z-degrees. These are essentially full degree programs that make course materials available to students at no cost. More and more institutions, especially on the community college level, are exploring this option in an attempt to address affordability of higher education.

There have been national initiatives to support colleges in offering Z-degrees. Nearly half of all states have considered OER legislation in past years, and it has increasingly become a go-to strategy for legislators seeking to make college education more affordable and effective. States can catalyze and support action at institutions by providing resources, incentives, and policy frameworks. Some of the more widely known system or consortia OER initiatives include the Community College Consortium for OER and Affordable Learning Georgia. With over half of all states having considered OER legislation in recent years, the OER State Policy Playbook (https://sparcopen.org/our-work/oer-state-policy-playbook/) was developed to offer guidance and policy recommendations.

Some schools have had to move away from a commitment to 100% OER because of the difficulties in replacing all content. However, they maintain a similar goal by continuing to advocate for more affordable learning materials.

Benefits of OER for Students

In many of the promotional materials and arguments for OER, cost is given as one of the main reasons behind the OER movement, use, and adoption. A 2018 study reports that students could be saving anywhere from $66 to $121 per course (Colvard, Watson, & Park) when OER are used instead of traditional commercial textbooks. This reflects the reality of higher education today, in which only a small percentage of college students are able to afford costly learning materials. According to many reports and observations in the *Chronicle of Higher Ed* (Blumenstyk, 2017; McMurtrie, 2019) and the *2018 Babson Survey Research Group Report* (Seaman & Seaman, 2018), a substantial number of college students have not even purchased a textbook for a particular course because they found it too expensive. Additionally, one in five college students has skipped or deferred a class due to the price of the required learning resources (Cengage Learning, 2016). These figures do not even take into consideration students who share, illegally copy, or hoard copies in the library reserve room. Bret Maney, Assistant Professor of English at Lehman College, City University of New York (CUNY), shared his concerns about the high costs of textbooks,

> *I've always found textbook costs to be hideously exploitative of students, who are usually strapped for cash as it is. I always make an effort to choose course texts in my English classes judiciously. I search for low-cost editions, have adopted the next-to-last version of an anthology, which can usually be purchased as a used copy at a steep discount, and scan texts at the start of the semester when permissible under copyright law. So my interest in*

> *OER is a natural extension of these preexisting concerns about the costs of higher education that go beyond tuition.*

But the benefits of OER go beyond student savings. According to Colvard, Watson, and Park (2018), OER don't just save money for our students and remove barriers to degree attainment but also have the potential to improve end-of-course grades and reduce withdrawals, demonstrating that decreasing the cost does not need to come at the price of decreasing quality.

While many OER advocates speak to the need to lower the cost and enable access from the first day of class to learning materials, studies that examine the OER impact on student learning also report increased student engagement with OER in comparison with traditional textbooks, and consequently improved learning outcomes (Petrides, Jimes, Middleton-Detzner, Walling, & Weiss, 2011; Feldstein et al., 2012; Pitt, Ebrahimi, McAndrew, & Coughlan, 2013; Gil, Candelas, Jara, Garcia, & Torres, 2013; Hilton, Gaudet, Clark, Robinson, & Wiley, 2013; Lindshield & Adhikari, 2013; Bliss, Robinson, Hilton, & Wiley, 2013; Allen & Seaman, 2014; Hilton, 2016; Grewe & Davis, 2017). In Chapters 5 and 7, we will discuss the benefits of OER for students in more detail.

Bertrade Ngo-Ngijol Banoum, Chair, Department of Africana Studies/Director, Women's Studies Program at Lehman College, CUNY, highlighted some of the unexpected benefits of OER,

> *I teach courses in African Studies and Women's Studies which are interdisciplinary. Consequently, I have always found it difficult, if not impossible, to identify textbooks that cover all essential themes of any one of my courses. This shortcoming has meant asking students to purchase many textbooks and/or handing out plenty of supplemental materials. Open Educational Resources sounded like the perfect solution to this problem and I decided to invest my time and newly acquired skills to develop OER content for all my courses.*

> *A pleasant surprise was the wealth of high quality open educational resources that are available online, waiting to be discovered and used. With a prescribed textbook, I would not have found those texts. When I used to prescribe a textbook for a course, it was often easier to conveniently just use it. With a shift to OER, there has been greater ability for my students*

> *and me to solicit sources and resources for classes together, making teaching and learning more participatory.*
>
> *Shifting from textbooks to OER has allowed me and the students to draw on historical and contemporary bases of knowledge in an interdisciplinary, intersectional and transnational way. With a textbook, the epistemological vantage may be limited and limiting. For example, lessons on Chicana feminism, Mujerista feminism, African feminism, or Indigenous feminisms, often require a search outside of the textbook for supplemental readings, as the textbook just does not have anything germane to add to the conversation. In this way, OER has allowed for more syllabus versatility, flexibility, fluidity, and accessibility. I am creating a syllabus and finding relevant sources and resources to fulfill the course learning outcomes. I am no longer teaching to the textbook.*

Miriam Deutch, Associate Professor at the Brooklyn College Library, CUNY, bolsters this view:

> *Curation of course materials allows faculty to customize their course materials. Moreover, curation of course materials allows faculty to choose diverse course materials that support inclusive teaching—increasing awareness of diversity, including ethnicity, gender identity, race, (dis)abilities, equity, and religious values. It can also include multimedia that addresses a variety of learning approaches.*

Online and Course Design

OER have allowed faculty to share learning materials easily. A unique feature of OER is that they start as digital, which makes them much easier to share, though the final product does not have to be digital. This book assumes that OER are offered online as opposed to hard copy versions, even though students may have an option to print out or purchase hard copy versions of OER that otherwise live online. OER textbooks can be printed as well as any other text, and usually it is for a fraction of the price of the equivalent publisher's version. As the result of the OER's digital nature, online educators are frequently well prepared to become early adopters of OER, unless they are fully invested with a publisher. Often publishers provide more than just an electronic text and may also offer a fully developed online course with all the ancillary materials ready to be imported into a learning management system or hosted on the publisher's proprietary platform.

In many cases, the instructors of online and hybrid (aka blended) courses are the first ones at an institution to adopt OER, as faculty teaching in those formats are much more accustomed to using online resources. We would like to call this "OOER"—"online" open educational resources—where online is nearly synonymous with the concept of OER.

Since the majority of OER are delivered online, even a face-to-face course that uses OER digital material becomes in effect a hybrid course, making *online course design* an essential element in planning.

Another less obvious benefit is that faculty who use OER are likely to refresh and renew their course design, make their courses more relevant, and realign course materials with learning objectives, assignments, and activities. During this process, faculty often improve the learning experience for students. Though course design is not always present or apparent in conversations about OER, it is in fact at the core of OER success.

This should not be seen as a revolutionary or an uncommon phenomenon, as intentional course design is already acknowledged as being fundamental to the success of online and hybrid offerings, and there already exist well-established standards and quality criteria for online course design. Several rubrics and quality scorecards have been developed over the years to guide the process of course design. *Quality Matters Course Design Rubric Standards, Open SUNY Course Quality Review (OSCQR)*, the *Online Learning Consortium (OLC) Quality Course Teaching* and *Instructional Practice Scorecard* are among those rubrics most commonly used in the field of online education, outlining essential course elements that define quality course and instructional design.

Phylise Banner, Learning Experience Designer and Consultant, highlights the key role instructional design and instructional designers can play in supporting teaching and learning, *"My instructional design and technology expertise enable me to weave OER seamlessly into the learning experiences. Working with OER empowers faculty to contextualize and tailor content, interaction, and assessment to create a meaningful student experience."*

The Role of Faculty

Faculty are, and must remain, directly involved in the course design process as they are key players and stakeholders in the use, adoption, and creation of OER. When it comes to choosing course materials, faculty are usually the decision makers. The attractions of the traditional textbook are obvious, as Kim Grewe, Associate Professor of English and Instructional Technologist at Eastern Shore Community College, noted:

> *It is true that many commercial textbooks are visually appealing, provide practice exercises, thought exercises, and for the teachers, the ever-important and time-saving test banks and other ancillary materials. The material is usually high quality and the assessments carefully crafted and calibrated. They can save faculty a great deal of time. It is easy to rely on textbooks. Most faculty were taught using textbooks, so they like to use textbooks when they teach. Ironically, because textbooks cost so much and are required in a course, that is another reason faculty feel obligated to use them.*

While publishers have been adapting to market demands by creating digital learning materials that go beyond a traditional text, there is often as a lack of intentional planning and design with the diverse student populations in mind. Also, as the result of the OER movement, publishers have responded with new content access models. For example, they may offer a subscription or institutional membership that gives access to learning materials at a discounted price, potentially lowering the cost for students if all instructors at an institution use that publisher for course materials.

Faculty are quite pragmatic when it comes to the selection of learning materials. Coverage of course topics, quality of the materials, appropriateness for the student audience, and access and cost to the student are usually the main considerations for faculty. There is definitely a strong presence of what we call OER "purists" in the OER movement. An OER "purist" is someone who is not only a proponent of open pedagogy but also believes that course materials should be comprised *only* of OER materials, and many go beyond that to say that all OER should meet the conditions of the most unrestricted use (for example, to allow all remixing and derivative works). However, most faculty are not OER "purists."

While in some cases it might be possible for courses to use OER content exclusively, some courses might require a combination of OER and "free but not OER" materials. We have found that most faculty are concerned with lowering or eliminating cost to students while retaining the quality of their courses. This difference in approach by faculty, as compared to administrators and some OER proponents, can be due to the fact that OER initiatives are often spearheaded and led by those who might be less focused on navigating some of the teaching and learning issues that preoccupy faculty. Thus, in order for the OER initiatives to take off and be successful on a university campus, like any other strategic initiative, it is crucial to involve faculty from the very beginning. OER initiatives must include opportunities for faculty to share their successes and have established structures to ensure that faculty are supported and rewarded from the very start of the course planning processes.

References

Allen, E., & Seaman, J. (2014). *Opening the curriculum: Open educational resources in U.S.* Retrieved from www.onlinelearningsurvey.com/reports/openingthecurriculum2014.pdf

Bliss, T., Robinson, T. J., Hilton, J., & Wiley, D. (2013). An OER COUP: College teacher and student perceptions of open educational resources. *Journal of Interactive Media in Education, 17*(1), 1–25.

Blumenstyk, G. (2017). Publishers and open-resource advocates square off on the future of course content. *The Chronicle of Higher Education.* Retrieved from www.chronicle.com/article/PublishersOpen-Resource/239806

Cengage Learning. (2016). *Open educational resources (OER) and the evolving higher education landscape.* Retrieved from http://assets.cengage.com/pdf/wp_oer-evolving-higher-ed-landscape.pdf

Colvard, N. B., Watson, C. E., & Park, H. (2018). The impact of open educational resources on various student success metrics. *International Journal of Teaching and Learning in Higher Education, 30*(2), 262–276.

EDUCAUSE Learning Initiative (ELI). (2018a). *7 things you should know about open education: Practices.* Retrieved from https://library.educause.edu/-/media/files/library/2018/7/eli7158.pdf

EDUCAUSE Learning Initiative (ELI). (2018b). *7 things you should know about open education: Content.* Retrieved from https://library.educause.edu/resources/2018/6/7-things-you-should-know-about-open-education-content

EDUCAUSE Learning Initiative (ELI). (2018c). *7 things you should know about open education: Policies.* Retrieved from https://library.educause.edu/resources/2018/8/7-things-you-should-know-about-open-education-policies

Feldstein, A., Martin, M., Hudson, A., Warren, K., Hilton, J., & Wiley, D. (2012). Open textbooks and increased student access and outcomes. *European Journal of Open, Distance and E-Learning*. http://www.eurodl.org/materials/contrib/2012/Feldsteint_et_al.pdf

Gil, P., Candelas, F., Jara, C., Garcia, G., & Torres, F. (2013). Web-based OERs in computer networks. *International Journal of Engineering Education, 29*(6), 1537–1550.

Grewe, K., & Davis, W. P. (2017). The impact of enrollment in an OER course on student learning outcomes. *The International Review of Research in Open and Distributed Learning, 18*(4). doi:10.19173/irrodl.v18i4.2986

Griffiths, R., Gardner, S., Lundh, P., Shear, L., Ball, A., Mislevy, J., . . . Staisloff, R. (2018). *Participant experiences and financial impacts: Findings from year 2 of achieving the dream's OER degree initiative.* Menlo Park, CA: SRI International.

Hewlett Foundation. (n.d.). *Open educational resources.* Retrieved from https://hewlett.org/strategy/open-educational-resources/

Hilton, J. (2016). Open educational resources and college textbook choices: A review of research on efficacy and perceptions. *Educational Technology Research and Development, 64*(4), 573–590.

Hilton, J., Gaudet, D., Clark, P., Robinson, J., & Wiley, D. (2013). The adoption of open educational resources by one community college math department. *The International Review of Research in Open and Distance Learning, 14*(4), 37–50.

Lindshield, B., & Adhikari, K. (2013). Online and campus college students like using an open educational resource instead of a traditional textbook. *Journal of Online Learning & Teaching, 9*(1), 1–7. Retrieved from http://jolt.merlot.org/vol9no1/lindshield_0313.htm

McMurtrie, B. (2019). Professors worry about the cost of textbooks, but free alternatives pose their own problems. *The Chronicle of Higher Education*. Retrieved from www.chronicle.com/article/Professors-Worry-About-the/245435

Petrides, L., Jimes, C., Middleton-Detzner, C., Walling, J., & Weiss, S. (2011). Open textbook adoption and use: Implications for teachers and learners. *Open Learning, 26*(1), 39–49.

Pitt, R., Ebrahimi, N., McAndrew, P., & Coughlan, T. (2013). Assessing OER impact across organisations and learners: Experiences from the bridge to success project. *Journal of Interactive Media in Education* (3). Retrieved from http://jime.open.ac.uk/article/view/2013-17/501

Seaman, J. E., & Seaman, J. (2018). *Freeing the textbook: Open education resources in U.S. higher education.* Babson Survey Research Group. Retrieved from www.onlinelearningsurvey.com/reports/freeingthetextbook2018.pdf

Wiley, D. (2018). *The OER adoption impact calculator*, version 1.2. Retrieved from http://impact.lumenlearning.com/

Young, J. (2018). *Free textbooks are not always free: New study analyzes OER's costs to colleges.* Retrieved from www.edsurge.com/news/2018-10-18-free-textbooks-are-not-always-free-new-study-analyzes-oer-s-costs-to-colleges

Chapter 2

Before You Begin
The OER Essentials

First, let's dig into the definition of open educational resources (OER), which are "high-quality teaching, learning, and research materials that are free for people everywhere to use and repurpose," as defined by the Hewlett Foundation (n.d., para. 1). These are digital teaching and learning materials that have been made available for free use and/ or are in the public domain and, depending on the licensing rules set by the creator of the materials, can potentially be shared, adapted, and remixed with other materials and redistributed. Another way to think of OER is to dissect the acronym as follows: *open*, that is, openly licensed so you can retain, reuse, revise, remix, and redistribute— the 5Rs (Wiley, n.d., Defining the "Open" in Open Content and Open Educational Resources section, para. 1); *educational*, meaning designed for educational use; and *resources*, meaning materials that support teaching and learning, including textbooks, video, quizzes, and more. A simple way to understand the concept of the 5Rs is that they encompass all the activities you can potentially engage in with OER. The 5Rs are defined by Wiley (n.d., Defining the "Open" in Open Content and Open Educational Resources section, para. 1) as follows:

1) *Retain—the right to make, own, and control copies of the content (e.g., download, duplicate, store, and manage)*
2) *Reuse—the right to use the content in a wide range of ways (e.g., in a class, in a study group, on a website, in a video)*
3) *Revise—the right to adapt, adjust, modify, or alter the content itself (e.g., translate the content into another language)*
4) *Remix—the right to combine the original or revised content with other material to create something new (e.g., incorporate the content into a mashup)*

5) *Redistribute—the right to share copies of the original content, your revisions, or your remixes with others (e.g., give a copy of the content to a friend)*

These 5Rs are essential to understanding what you can do with OER and the flexibility you can have when working with OER learning materials to support student learning. OER licensing conditions, as provided by Creative Commons, give a clearer indication to faculty of what they can and can't do when handling OER content. When content is not explicitly marked as public domain or with an OER license clearly affixed, faculty sometimes are unsure whether and how they can use particular resources and how to share them with students. Creative Commons licenses provide more specific information on the terms of use and can also indicate whether and what sort of modifications can be made.

Depending on the specifics of the licensing, there are several variables and parameters for OER use, ranging from using and sharing free of charge while simply giving attribution to the creator, to freely remixing and adapting content as you wish. If an academic article is clearly marked as downloadable and usable for educational purposes, an instructor can feel free to not only link to it but also to display the article in a learning management system (LMS), perhaps making it easier for students to access it more expeditiously. For example, articles from open access journals can be crucial for keeping students abreast of the latest and most relevant scholarship in their field and can augment what can be provided via the library's e-reserve. Note that articles in open access journals might still bear a copyright notice by a particular article's author. This means that the article may be free to read and usually free to download but must be correctly attributed to the author and cannot be altered in any way.

Copyright, Public Domain, and Creative Commons Licenses

There are three main categories that will help you differentiate between how you can use published work. These are the traditional copyright, public domain, and Creative Commons licenses.

One of the misconceptions is that anything that you find on the internet is readily accessed and permissible to use in any way you like in your course. Whether you are an instructor or serve in a faculty support role, you might want to get familiar with the types of licensing conditions or terms of use to better understand what you can and cannot do. See if your institution has developed or adopted frequently asked questions for content use or can guide you through the complexities of the terms of use. Librarians are a great resource to assist you in determining the licensing conditions—do not hesitate to make use of their expertise. Even though faculty might be attuned to some of the rules and guidelines, at times it is not so easy to decipher the specifics of the authorship, terms of use, and licensing.

A common mistake made by some faculty wishing to use video or feature films is to assume that all of these are free to download from the internet and then upload to their own LMS, or that those posting videos necessarily had the rights to do so. In fact, many videos are not clearly marked as to rights, and therefore it is wise to only link to the original sources rather than download the video (aka create a copy of the content). Further, it is best to assume that these videos might disappear and the links become broken in the event that the actual rights holder requests that the hosting platform take them down.

Traditional copyright means that the work cannot be used, adapted, copied, or published without the proper permission. Furthermore, even if it does not bear a copyright notice, under U.S. law, all original work is automatically protected under copyright when created. However, there are many complexities concerning use in an educational context. For the most recent laws, rules, and regulations, you might want to check out the United States Copyright Office website or your institutional site on this topic, if one exists.

Just as instructors have to ensure that their students submit original work, give credit to other people's ideas and demonstrate academic integrity, citing properly and providing attributions, this is also an essential skill for instructors to have when working with OER.

Proper attribution can become rather complicated with remixed OER—that is, OER coming from different sources but presented as one entity. It isn't always enough to just list all the sources at the end, as this could be quite misleading. For example, if source A is used for 80% of your new text, with 10% contributed by source B and the final 10% by yourself, the proper attributions could be quite confusing. You can liken this to a situation in which you had a conversation with two different people that you repeated to a third party—in an attempt to summarize you may combine what the two parties said without distinguishing between their respective contributions. This might send a misleading message to someone unaware of the distinctions of those two parties' views. This is especially fraught when the value and significance of the different contributions vary greatly. For example, suppose you merged passages from Jane Austen with Jane Austen fan fiction. Even if both were in the public domain, you would still want to give clear attributions to distinguish these two contributors and different sources.

Those in academia might already be familiar with the Teach Act of 2002, which was an amendment to copyright law. There are many sites that provide good explanations of the Teach Act and how it pertains to educational use. One of these that does a good job of simplifying matters is the Copyright Crash Course site at the University of Texas (https://guides.lib.utexas.edu/copyright/teachact).

While the Teach Act was meant to cover the use of copyrighted works in a face-to-face setting, as well as those digital materials in distance education, there are still some differences in the respective permissions for use in one or the other format, with more allowance made for face-to-face delivery. Because these rules of the Teach Act are often difficult to interpret in a particular case, one can often more reliably follow the principles of fair use.

In academia, the notion of fair use is frequently applied to enable the use of copyrighted works to support student learning, under certain limited circumstances and subject to certain constraints. Miriam Deutch, Associate Professor at the Brooklyn College Library, CUNY, describes how in her role as a librarian she helps faculty identify, evaluate, and facilitate secure access to different types of learning materials, including those provided under fair use:

> *There are so many faculty that I work with to curate openly available resources and/or library licensed resources. I also remind and guide faculty to professional organizations, institutes, and associations in their field that provide openly available content in a variety of mediums. Many faculty are unaware of these resources. In addition, I frequently assist faculty with evaluating whether their use of a book chapter or journal article constitutes fair use. If so, we password protect that document so only the persons enrolled in the course are able to view the text.*

There are many websites that lay out the conditions for fair use. One of these is the University of Texas Copyright Crash Course site's section on Fair Use and the Four Factor test (https://guides.lib.utexas.edu/copyright/fairuse). Stanford University Libraries also has a great resource page of copyright and fair use Charts and Tools (http://fairuse.stanford.edu/library-resources/) that contain many infographics and checklists you can use to determine the status of materials.

As you might know, not everything is covered by copyright. This includes facts, discoveries, and ideas and U.S. government works, to name just a few. These works, along with those formerly under copyright but for which copyright has expired, are known as works in the public domain. The public domain status enables you and your students to use many of these works to support teaching, learning, and scholarship. It may mean you can assign an early-twentieth-century novel to read without students incurring the cost of a book. Or it may mean you can ask students to review documents on the Library of Congress website or in the National Archives. However, even on government sites, it is necessary to read the fine print. For example, the Library of Congress site has been given the right to post some valuable materials still under copyright—such materials can still be linked to and reviewed by students on the Library of Congress website but cannot be freely remixed or redistributed by you.

Public domain, which is now generally included in the definition of OER, is work that can be used and repurposed without any restrictions or the need for permissions. It applies to works published prior to 1923, work that is no longer under copyright, or work that creators have deliberately placed in the public domain. In 2019, a large trove of works created in 1923 finally entered the public domain. These include such works as Virginia Woolf's *Jacob's Room* and Robert Frost's poem collection, *New Hampshire*. Unfortunately, unlike intentionally labeled OER, public domain is not always clearly identified as such.

Sites such as Public Domain Review (https://publicdomainreview.org) provide collections, links, and other resources as well as updates to assist you in finding public domain works. Faculty teaching the humanities, legal studies, history, political science, and many other fields often make use of public domain works, tapping public domain resource collections such as Project Gutenberg, HathiTrust, and the Internet Archive. These all include texts not only in English but also many in translation, which have been made freely available. They may also include other types of materials in the public domain. Those teaching immigration law or nursing or science might find public domain works on various government sites.

It is important to remember that while the original text may be in the public domain, derivatives or the new iterations of the work may not be in the public domain. For example, those teaching classes with works by Shakespeare are likely familiar with the public domain copies available online for these texts. But there may also be books on Shakespeare that are not in the public domain—these would include annotated versions or those containing essays or explications of themes and passages. Remember that once something is in the public domain, an author can create new works or versions that are not in the public domain.

Again, it might not be easy to identify if the works are in the public domain, so be sure to intentionally search for the terms of use or other notices that might identify the nature of that content. Librarians can be particularly helpful in deciphering and tracking down the owners, various permissions and rights. They can tell you not only how to attribute the work but how you might use it.

While not all OER material bears a Creative Commons license, it is true that all material that bears a Creative Commons license is OER. The principle behind Creative Commons licenses is that work may be used without permission, but only under certain circumstances. Creators set rules for the way their work can be used (Creative Commons, n.d.). When you use works with a Creative Commons license, once you become familiar with the basic attribution terminology, you are equipped with more exact and clear knowledge of what you can do with the work, because the conditions of use are clearly specified. Simply put, the licenses range from being completely open to ones that have more restrictions. The Creative Commons website (https://creativecommons.org/licenses/) offers a detailed description of all types of licenses:

Attribution—CC BY
This license lets others distribute, remix, tweak, and build upon your work, even commercially, as long as they credit you for the original creation. This is the most accommodating of licenses offered. Recommended for maximum dissemination and use of licensed materials.

Attribution-ShareAlike—CC BY-SA

This license lets others remix, tweak, and build upon your work even for commercial purposes, as long as they credit you and license their new creations under the identical terms. This license is often compared to "copyleft" free and open source software licenses. All new works based on yours will carry the same license, so any derivatives will also allow commercial use. This is the license used by Wikipedia, and is recommended for materials that would benefit from incorporating content from Wikipedia and similarly licensed projects.

Attribution-NoDerivs—CC BY-ND

This license allows for redistribution, commercial and non-commercial, as long as it is passed along unchanged and in whole, with credit to you.

Attribution-NonCommercial—CC BY-NC

This license lets others remix, tweak, and build upon your work non-commercially, and although their new works must also acknowledge you and be non-commercial, they don't have to license their derivative works on the same terms.

Attribution-NonCommercial-ShareAlike—CC BY-NC-SA

This license lets others remix, tweak, and build upon your work non-commercially, as long as they credit you and license their new creations under the identical terms.

Attribution-NonCommercial-NoDerivs—CC BY-NC-ND

This license is the most restrictive of our six main licenses, only allowing others to download your works and share them with others as long as they credit you, but they can't change them in any way or use them commercially.

To understand what this all means, let's take a look at a hypothetical case of a Professor Banks teaching business ethics. Professor Banks has found both clearly labeled OER materials and also other materials that are available on the internet but for which there are no clearly defined terms of usage. One of the materials he has found is a case history presented in a peer-reviewed online journal for which Professor Banks' school library has a subscription. He can add a direct link to this library periodical in his online class site. He has also found a Ted Talk that bears a Creative Commons license indicating he is free to embed the video in his class—while the video is actually remaining on the TEDTalk site, students are able to play it within the LMS of the class site. The professor has also located an open textbook that clearly indicates that the professor can not only freely use but can also remix the content with his own supplementary commentary. Professor Banks therefore makes it available as a PDF in the LMS, and simply provides a proper attribution for that material.

However, the professor also finds that someone has posted a PBS video on YouTube that matches up well with an ethical problem that is the topic of discussion for one of the weeks of the course. Because the video appears to be uploaded by a third party, and Professor Banks is unsure about whether that entity had the right to do so, he decides to only link to it and also makes provision for a backup video in case the original selection happens to disappear. Professor Banks provides the attribution for the video to PBS and the original creators whose notice appears in the video itself.

Furthermore, Professor Banks wants to use about 200 words from a well-known book on business ethics that is still under copyright by an author who is a recognized authority on a topic featured in another week of his course. While the library possesses a hard copy of the book, there is no digitized version. Moreover, the 200 words are comprised of two quotations from different parts of the book. Because the amount that the professor wants to quote constitutes a very small part of the 300-page book (meeting fair use guidelines), Professor Banks will use the quotations in the weekly online lecture, clearly labeling each with a full citation and reference to the two chapters from which the quotes came.

Finally, Professor Banks will forgo using a recent article from a periodical that is behind a paywall and to which the university does not provide access in favor of an article from a daily newspaper that his university has arranged to make freely available online to all registered students.

As these examples illustrate, it is essential to learn about all these types of permissions as well as the different OER licenses so that you can more easily make informed decisions about how to handle your course content selections. Resource or copyright librarians are often the go-to people for questions related to copyright, licensing, permissions, and OER. They are often asked to "decode" licenses and explain in plain English the terms of use and how the terminology of OER licenses actually apply. These expert librarians can also assist faculty with finding course-specific materials and ensure that faculty comply with the license terms and conditions.

Types of Materials and Where to Find Them

When OER sprang to life years ago, the types of OER were more limited in variety and scope. Since then, the range and diversity of materials has been incrementally expanding. These now range from full courses, course materials, lesson plans, open textbooks, videos, and images, to software and other types of ancillary materials. The latter include course discussion questions, course assignments, quizzes and tests, digital simulations, and games.

Bertrade Ngo-Ngijol Banoum, Chair at the Department of Africana Studies and Director of the Women's Studies Program at Lehman College, CUNY, reflected on the diversity of materials available:

> *A major surprise was finding an essential resource in a most unlikely website or finding links to various resources from one source. Use of OER has yielded the comparative advantage of allowing easy online access to different types of resources on a single platform—classic and current texts from trailblazing/widely read and emerging feminist scholars, activists and writers, personal narratives, current events articles, poems, songs, artwork, blogs, TED Talks, documentary films, video clips, story maps, radio recordings and social media input.*

Where is the best place to find OER? Knowing the answer could save infinite hours of work by faculty, librarians, course developers, instructional designers, and students. Unfortunately, discoverability is one of the major challenges of working with OER. While there are various types of repositories or aggregators, and even some sites that attempt to provide meta searches that facilitate that process of searching and filtering through the wealth of resources, there is simply no one place to go to find all OER.

Librarians are uniquely qualified to help faculty identify suitable resources for their courses. Miriam Deutch, Associate Professor at the Brooklyn College Library, CUNY, described a few different cases in which she assisted faculty in curating OER content:

I worked with a philosophy professor who replaced a textbook with OER. Initially, he had some difficulty identifying modern translations of philosophy works. He and many other professors prefer modern translations because it makes the text more accessible to students. We were able to curate sufficient readings by identifying library e-books, by scanning a small portion of a print book that qualified as fair use, and adding links to the openly available Stanford Encyclopedia of Philosophy and Internet Encyclopedia of Philosophy.

In another case, we sought to find modern translations for Classics courses, which was also a challenge. The professor evaluated some Wikipedia articles and I also helped to secure access to library e-books, and purchased licenses that allowed for unlimited use. This was particularly important since the professor teaches large enrollment courses. We also identified texts in Project Gutenberg, freely available e-books on the University of California Press website, the Oxford Companion of Ancient Greece and Rome, as well as texts from Poetry in Translation, a digital publisher providing modern, high quality open access translations of classic texts.

In another instance, I worked with a communications professor whose OER is a mix of library resources and openly available resources from sites such as the National Institute on Deafness and Other Communication Disorders. The professor also used portions from Wikibooks, and integrated authoritative videos and podcasts from sources such as PBS, BBC, and TED Talks.

In my work with faculty, I often emphasize the inclusion of multimedia in OER because it illustrates concepts in ways text cannot. Multimedia also can make courses more engaging. OER development at Brooklyn College has also inspired greater use of a variety of digital tools such as text annotation software, mapping software such as ARGIS Story Maps and Google Maps, as well as video and audio assignments.

OER that are appropriate for your course may be found in a number of ways, but perhaps it is easiest to think of three major types of destinations to find OER. First, there are general collections or repositories, which may be further subdivided into discipline-based subject categories. Some repositories are linked to large-scale initiatives that are grant-funded or statewide efforts. Second, there are discipline-based, topical, or specialized interest collections. Some of the latter category are limited to one type of resource, such as textbooks, while others include everything from courses, videos, and images to full textbooks. Most are targeted to higher education, though some also include resources for the K-12 level or professional development. Third, there are meta sites that search across different types of repositories to facilitate and simplify the process for the user. Additionally, many institutional libraries have started to develop their own discipline-specific collections, based on the work they have done while assisting faculty (often utilizing the LibGuide platform). For a list of repositories, visit the authors' website.

It is also important not to discount the value of a Google search—by inputting the subject specific keywords and adding OER to your search, you might find a wealth of resources. Furthermore, by using the advanced search options, you can filter for various licensing conditions. It is sometimes possible to find something through an advanced Google search that is not discoverable in any other way. One thing to keep in mind is that even if you filter the Google results, selecting only for royalty-free materials, you still need to individually double-check the licensing conditions for each, as in some cases the licensing conditions might not be clearly noted or readily identifiable. Also, be aware that those items that are not clearly licensed might not be recognized by the search engine. Therefore, it might be a good idea to compare the search results with and without filtering by the license type.

For any type of search you make, try to broaden your search and then narrow it, or vice versa—make it very specific and then broaden the terms. For example, when you are looking for Shakespeare's play "Hamlet," depending on what you are looking for, you might want to broaden the search and look for "English Literature OER," "Elizabethan Drama OER," "Shakespeare OER," or, more narrowly, "original Hamlet OER." Be prepared to be surprised—depending on your discipline you may be overwhelmed by a large number of resources or puzzled by the lack thereof. As you conduct your search, keep a good list of evaluation criteria handy to help you navigate and assess your findings. You can start with the OER Evaluation and Selection Criteria (see Figure 2.1) created by the authors of this book, or develop your own list.

Remember also that new OER resources are created every day—search results found yesterday might prove different or better if you search again today. You can stay up-to-date with new developments by signing up for notifications. While you may be familiar with signing up for newsletters or live notifications from social media channels, specific users, or organizations, you can also sign up for a content-change detection service. While there are paid versions of this kind of service, you may also sign up for a free version called Google Alerts. It allows you to set notification preferences, choosing the frequency of notifications, type of source, and region of origin, as well as define the type of results to either include all sources or to narrow the results to display only the best.

At the time of the writing of this book, no central repository exists for all OER. Anne Rice, Assistant Professor, Africana Studies and Women's Studies at Lehman College, CUNY, commented on this issue,

> *There is no central repository for Africana OER resources, which means that it is very time-consuming finding resources after 1940 or so. I already knew that many texts no longer subject to copyright were readily available in online archives such as Schomburg and Project Gutenberg. Chapters of other texts were available from archives of magazines such as the Atlantic and the New Yorker, where they had been originally published. However, there were almost no Africana literature resources available in OER repositories.*

Luckily, more and more search engines are becoming available to simplify and aid in this complex journey. Aggregators like Oasis (https://oasis.geneseo.edu/) or Mason OER Metafinder (https://oer.deep webaccess.com/oer/desktop/en/search.html) most closely approach a metasearch capability and are specifically developed for the purpose of easing the search for OER, allowing one to filter and search across several OER repositories. They enable you to broaden or narrow your search, often by the type of OER—whether a textbook, a course, interactive simulations, audiobooks, videos, podcasts, public domain books, or learning objects. You can also apply parameters for the date the OER was created or to select which repositories to search across.

Before you begin your search, think about what you are looking for as this makes it easier to identify the search engine or the type of repository that would be most helpful. For example, if you are looking for an open textbook, you might head straight to the open textbook repositories. One of these is the Open Textbook Library (https://open.umn.edu/opentextbooks/), offering textbooks from various sources and in many disciplines. Additionally, the Open Textbook Library provides detailed peer reviews that often further address some of the teaching issues you may be concerned with—for example, noting whether the open textbook covers certain topics in depth, whether a quiz bank is included, or whether the charts and illustrations constitute a particularly valuable feature of the book. So if one were looking for a textbook in introductory statistics, one would find multiple versions but perhaps choose one that has been highly rated by peer reviews and/or one with some ancillary resources included.

Again, as you set upon your mission to find high-quality learning materials, don't discount your institutional support systems. Librarians are trained researchers, equipped with a skill set to search across various databases, including the complex ones that exist for OER. Instructional designers and technologists also may have specialized knowledge of OER. We will address various support systems in more detail in Chapter 8.

Bertrade Ngo-Ngijol Banoum, Chair at the Department of Africana Studies and Director of the Women's Studies Program at Lehman College, CUNY, recounted her search process:

> *The starting point for each one of my OER was my syllabus, including course goals and learning outcomes. The next step was searching for scholarly open access materials for every course unit. This was a time-consuming process with many trials and errors but a very rewarding one. While license attribution was clear for some of the resources identified, it was not obvious for others, so I sought assistance from Lehman College*

librarians. For must-read texts in Women's Studies that were not available in the public domain, protected access was granted through the library, and they also ordered a few e-books for me in the process.

Evaluating and Selecting OER

Not all OER that you will find might be worth adopting. In fact, quality can vary quite a bit. That is why OER repositories like Open Textbook Library or Merlot (www.merlot.org) that provide peer reviews, ratings or curated lists by recognized authorities can be of such value. Unfortunately, in most cases it might be up to you and your colleagues to evaluate the OER for yourselves.

Consider utilizing a list of criteria for evaluating and selecting OER or establishing your own to meet your needs. For sample evaluation rubrics and checklists see the authors' OER Evaluation and Selection Criteria (Figure 2.1) in this book or visit the authors' website.

The basic criteria for any list should address the broad categories of quality, such as the comprehensiveness of the text and its accuracy and appropriateness for students. More specific criteria might relate to alignment with course goals and unit learning objectives. Additional criteria might involve technical characteristics such as accessibility and/or interactivity. Some OER might have been created with industry standards and quality criteria already in mind. On the other hand, you might come across OER that don't meet the level of excellence that you might expect. Thus, before deciding to adopt specific OER, it is essential to conduct a careful and diligent evaluation.

Evaluating Open Textbooks

When faculty choose their textbook, they generally might have a mental checklist of criteria. This checklist might focus on areas such as content, design, and cost. Some publishers offer a variety of online resources to accompany their texts. These resources are intended to lift the burden of some instructional tasks such as creation of visual materials, lectures, tests and quizzes, etc. The basic criteria used to evaluate traditional textbooks can also be used to evaluate open textbooks, but there might be additional criteria that might be of importance in regard to the online modality or the conditions for use.

This list of criteria is suitable for any type of OER, including an open textbook or individual OER artifacts/objects. This guide is intended for individual faculty or those supporting them. Not all criteria will apply in every case, but the criteria can serve as a general framework for the evaluation and selection process. Depending on the subject or course material you already have, or what you are seeking, one or more of these criteria may be more important or have greater priority.

Coverage, Context, Comprehensiveness

— Does the content cover the topic(s) being considered?
— Is the context appropriate for the approach to the subject matter?
— Is the content adequate to address the topic/s or issue/s, time-period, perspectives?
— Does it stand on its own, or need additional content in the form of other materials or instructor commentary, etc.?

Quality, Reliability, Currency

— Is the content clear, well-written, and readable? Is the content accurate and free of biases, errors, or mistakes (grammatical, technical, or informational)?
— Is the source reputable or peer reviewed? Are the authors recognized in their field?
— Is the content current? If not current, is the content still meaningful, relevant, or significant for your course/unit/topic?

Appropriateness for Course Level, Student Audience, Learning Outcome(s)

— Are the language and the approach appropriate and inclusive of the target audience? (undergraduate or graduate, lower-level or upper level, subject major or general audience, etc.)
— Does the content align well with one or more learning outcomes?
— Is the content free of cultural biases and stereotypes? In not, can instructor commentary or other content serve to offset or provide more inclusive perspectives?

Figure 2.1 OER Evaluation and Selection Criteria

Access, Accessibility, Format

— Is the content easy to access? Is it in a usable format as is? Is the content easy to navigate, save or print?
— Can it be made available for use offline? Can it be downloaded/ uploaded independently of the original location?
— Does the content meet accessibility requirements? If not, can one easily make appropriate changes or transform it into another medium, if desired? Consult your institutional standards or the OER Accessibility Toolkit (https://open.ubc.ca/teach/ oer-accessibility-toolkit/).

Adaptable, Customizable, Open vs Free-to-Use

— Is it easy to adopt just a portion of the content? Can it meaningfully be combined or assembled with other materials? Does it complement other materials for the course/unit?
— Does the content fit well into the structure of a course assignment(s), activity(ies), etc.? Does the instructor need to make course modifications to accommodate the new content?
— Do the licensing conditions allow for needed modifications? Does the content bear an open (Creative Commons) license or a statement indicating the terms of use as free or free with conditions? Does it allow for download and reuse (making a copy), or can you only link to it?

Supplementary or Time-Saving Resources (if preferred or needed)

— Are there student resources like online labs, simulations, images and videos, self-paced practice or assessment activities to support learning?
— Are there accompanying materials such as test banks, homework problems, instructor guides, slides and handouts, case studies, or multimedia content to support instruction?

Zhadko, O. & Ko, S. (2019, August 27). Evaluation and Selection Criteria for OER. Retrieved from https://oerworkshop.commons. gc.cuny.edu/

Figure 2.1 OER Evaluation and Selection Criteria

As Anne Rice, Assistant Professor, Africana Studies and Women's Studies at Lehman College, commented on her evaluation of OER, *"Because I am dealing primarily with literary texts, I evaluated OER texts using the same standards I would for traditionally published texts. I only used academic and respected journalism sources."*

Some additional criteria for OER evaluation might be the cost or document type (PDF, online, ePub), the ability to print, hosting platform, meaningful, reliable reviews and ratings, and licensing conditions.

As you know, there is no ideal textbook. Some disciplines are more likely to have an established or more standardized course outline and content—like introductory biology, chemistry, or American history—while others like contemporary politics or digital marketing have to rely more heavily on current media or industry-specific content. This highlights the importance of using an evaluation checklist to guide your selection process when choosing OER for your course.

In Chapter 3, we will take a closer look at the decision-making process regarding adopting existing resources and creating your own.

References

Creative Commons. (n.d.). *About the licenses*. Retrieved from https://creativecommons.org/licenses/

Hewlett Foundation. (n.d.). *Open educational resources*. Retrieved from https://hewlett.org/strategy/open-educational-resources/

Wiley, D. (n.d.). *Defining the "open" in open content and open educational resources*. Retrieved from https://opencontent.org/definition/

Part II

Course Design

Chapter 3

Adopting, Adapting, and Authoring

There are three approaches you can take when working with OER: first, adopt and use OER as is; second, remix or assemble a variety of resources and adapt; and third, create new OER. Of course, as part of customizing to adapt, you may also author some new OER to fill in the gaps and provide contextual commentary. When authoring completely new OER content, you are likely to be taking on a bigger task. Sometimes these categories of working with OER overlap, especially in the online course environment where faculty are often responsible for course development.

How should one decide what is the best option? The simple answer to this question would be—it depends. It depends on the discipline and how broad or narrow your course topics are. It might also depend on your technical expertise, how much time you have to devote to curating course materials or creating OER, and the support systems you have in place to help shoulder the burden. If you found it difficult to find just one traditional textbook to cover your course subject matter, you might find you have the same problem finding one OER text that will suffice. Naturally, courses that are based on contemporary events and issues might be good candidates for creating your own OER, mainly because of the subject's currency and changing nature. On the other hand, if your students have free access via the institution to mainstream news sources, and the subject is one that is ephemeral or constantly in flux, you might find it easier to simply point them to recent articles each semester.

General education curriculum might seem like a good choice for which to create OER, mainly because its nature is to be stable and ubiquitous, for example, an algebra course or an introduction to chemistry. It is likely that an OER textbook might already have been created in that subject, and you could readily adopt or adapt it through mixing with some of your own content or other resources. Finding a good textbook (OER or free-but-not-OER) that meets your course learning outcomes and covers most of the same content might feel like winning a lottery (that is, when you don't have to spend hours looking for additional learning materials or creating learning guides or lectures).

While some faculty might be able find an entire open textbook that meets all their course goals, others might have to mix and match from a variety of sources and create their own collection of OER to meet their needs. Or they might find an open textbook that meets some of their requirements but still might have the need to supplement those materials.

Helen Chang, Assistant Adjunct Professor at Lehman College, CUNY, teaches political science courses and sought to replace her existing course materials with OER:

> *I was looking for a textbook and also interested in a reader of original research, primary sources, and news media articles. There was a clear winner among the textbooks from OpenStax, in terms of quality, timeliness and updates. I found two readers and some individual modules for particular topics, but nothing compelling to use that would replace my current reader or other non-textbook materials.*

> *I wanted to keep the course zero cost to students, but I couldn't find easy and comprehensive OER. Instead, for non-textbook materials, I searched for institutional resources that would be free to my students but not necessarily "pure" OER. I compiled peer reviewed articles from Academic Search, JSTOR, and the New York Times and Wall Street Journal (the latter two which were available in free accounts to all students at my institution), as well as free podcasts and videos available on YouTube.*

Decision Deliberations

A further challenge related to making your decision is finding OER of sufficiently high quality. In Chapter 2 we discussed some of the standards you might use in evaluating potential OER. If you are able to find quality learning materials for your course and use them as is, there is no need to spend time creating your own. It's really no different from the typical selection of a non-OER textbook in that if you are able to find a perfect text that meets your course goals and student learning outcomes, you don't have to further deliberate and you can simply choose to adopt that text. Of course, you might have to think twice if the textbook is expensive and your students might not be able to afford it. You are even aware that if it is too expensive, a large proportion of your students will opt to not even purchase it—a less than ideal learning situation!

It's important that faculty not feel pressured by their institutions into accepting OER that do not meet the same standards as what they would normally choose for their students. While OER has become a social justice issue, those who want to ensure equality of education should not do so by adopting a lower standard for those student populations that are struggling with the costs of textbooks. But before concluding that there are no adequate OER or free-but-not-OER solutions, it is necessary to conduct a thorough and exhaustive search. Some ideas for how to go about this are discussed in Chapter 2 and also in this chapter. Bertrade Ngo-Ngijol Banoum, Chair at the Department of Africana Studies and Director of the Women's Studies Program at Lehman College, CUNY, reflected on the availability of materials: "*It has been challenging to realize that an essential, must-read text is not available in the public domain. However, some materials with copyright restrictions can be made available to our students through library e-reserves.*"

Choosing the perfect OER for your course might be more challenging that you might imagine, or just the opposite—it might be a lot easier than you thought. For some disciplines, you can readily find OER of comparable or, at times, higher quality than the traditional textbook, choosing from among the open textbooks and course specific collections of OER that are being created and shared. It's best to be mindful that the results of your OER searches might vary, depending on your course subject matter, your approach to the subject, or other factors. For example, perhaps you are teaching nineteenth-century English history, but you are seeking a text that takes on a social or economic approach rather than mainly a political history perspective. Or maybe you are teaching a personal finance course, but rather than using a text on the fundamentals of finance, you want something more in the vein of popular business books.

Perhaps you find one or more texts in the public domain rather than a recently created OER. Keeping in mind that material may be in the public domain because of its age, such texts may prove too outdated for your needs. For example, a translation of works from a foreign language made into English during the nineteenth century may be as nearly impenetrable for your students to understand as one in the original language! Or the text may include concepts and terminology or stereotypes that are no longer widely accepted or might even be judged objectionable by today's standards. Such a text might be suitable for an advanced class in which students are able to appraise the work in the context of others with which they are already familiar, but it may be entirely unsuitable and misleading for the purpose of introducing a lower-level class to the foundational concepts or basic knowledge of a subject.

Before you start considering creating your own OER, you should spend some time getting oriented with already existing resources, realizing that this is a rapidly evolving area and that new resources may have become available just a short time after your last search. For example, a faculty member teaching an economics course decides to explore OER because her current textbook is expensive and not particularly good. She is also concerned about the cost to her students, since in prior semesters many students skipped buying the textbook. Having taught her subject for several years, she has compiled a collection of resources that she regularly reviews before the semester's start and uses these to supplement the textbook. Following her colleague's advice, she searches for an open textbook and does not find many options. A few months later, after having consulted with a librarian at her school, she discovers a few options for her *Principles of Economics* course. She ends up adopting one of the OER textbooks after a careful review and continues to use a few of her previous resources to supplement the OER textbook.

Knowing how to conduct the search for OER content is essential. If you are new to this process, we do recommend that you spend some time developing this skill—it will pay off with dividends. First, be resourceful (see Chapters 2 and 8 for some ideas). Rather than just searching on your own, consider consulting with others at your institution (or even a colleague from another school) on the techniques they use to search and find OER in your discipline. Learn from those who have already walked this path. Second, as illustrated by the case of the economics professor, it is important to periodically repeat your search. OER development may be funded by the federal government, individual states, private foundations or schools, continually making new works available. Strategic investments into curriculum can result in the creation of open textbooks that may suddenly appear in one of your repeated searches.

If you decide to develop your own OER, consider whether you have time to keep resources up-to-date and current. If you rely heavily on an existing open textbook, then keeping up and reviewing a new edition would be no different than reviewing a new edition of a non-OER textbook. However, if you curate your learning materials and use multiple sources, then every semester you might have to schedule some time to revisit the original sources that you link to and ensure that the content has not disappeared or moved. For example, a faculty member teaching sociology might have adopted an OpenStax textbook and each week lists activities and provides direct links to readings. When a new edition of her OER textbook comes out and replaces the old one, the instructor discovers that all the links are broken and that she has to go back into the LMS and update every single hyperlink. If you aggregate and copy the content itself rather than just the links into a new document that is independent of the original source, you can avoid this issue of broken links. Of course, you must remember to provide all proper attributions for the content.

Even when you use a traditional text, you might be supplementing it with your own commentary, lectures, library reserves, and digital or other types of resources to provide additional context, demonstrate a concept, or just offer another perspective. You might use the same approach when you teach with OER and end up choosing one primary source and supplementing it with additional sources. At times, when you are not able to find OER that fully meet your course needs (or might not fully meet some criteria or a level of quality that is important to you), you might consider adopting just a portion of that OER and/or supplementing it with additional resources. You might also end up choosing an inexpensive textbook to provide the foundational knowledge on the subject and deliver all other course materials using OER and free-but-not-OER content, thus substantially reducing though not totally eliminating the cost to students. Such pragmatic approaches are sometimes necessary, especially in certain subject areas currently lacking sufficient and high-quality OER.

One of the authors of this book, Susan Ko, encountered this dilemma when developing new online courses on modern East Asia and Chinese civilization for her history department:

Although I conducted extensive searches, I was unable to find a textbook that covered the history of these regions in any sort of depth or breadth— nothing but a single chapter or two existed in any of the open textbooks. I have always found it helpful to have an anchor text that provided a framework and context for the students. In the past, when teaching these courses face-to-face, I would generally end up ordering two or three books for these classes—a main text plus a reading in social history and one in literature. I could no longer justify the rapidly spiraling costs to my students, and was determined to keep costs as low as possible.

I decided on one excellent textbook which sold for under $50, but one that I knew was readily available in inexpensive used copies, and even for rent from some booksellers. I then focused my time on finding the highest quality but freely available texts and resources to replace the additional content. I ended up with an eclectic group of sources, consisting of content openly licensed for use (true OER); those resources free to link to or download for educational use only, though otherwise under copyright; those literary and philosophical texts available under public domain; articles from news sources freely available to students at our institution; ebooks and full text articles available online through the library; links to special video lectures and presentations from various institutional and research organization sites; and finally, a grab-bag of publicly posted videos from YouTube. Last, I added my own commentary to supplement various topics and in response to student questions.

Since this was the first time I had used this particular mix of course materials, I surveyed my students in both classes via an anonymous online survey to ask them to rate the various types of content in regard to how helpful these were to their learning. I will be looking to the results of the survey to help me decide what materials to retain the next time I teach this course.

To select learning materials for your course, including primary and supplemental resources, you might want to use a course planning document to outline weekly learning objectives and outcomes, list instructional strategies to be used, identify assessment activities to enable students to demonstrate proficiency, and last but not least, to provide content or resources needed to support learning. Working on a course outline that includes all these elements requires time, diligence, and patience—and maybe a few revisions. We explain in detail how to go about this in Chapter 4.

Being Pragmatic About OER

As we stated in Chapter 2, "purity" of OER is one of the subjects often discussed by OER supporters and enthusiasts. Some are very strict about it—the "purists"—wanting to ensure that course learning materials are completely free both to students and an institution, while others think that as long as learning materials are free to students that is sufficient. Others will advocate only for those OER that are as openly licensed as possible, allowing for remixing and derivative works. But the majority of faculty are satisfied if the learning materials are free to students. Such faculty are happy to provide the stipulated attribution and are not concerned that the content licensing does not allow for a derivative work. Furthermore, as they collect and aggregate resources, the quality of learning materials is their top priority, and they end up supplementing existing resources with their own. Curtis Izen, Adjunct Lecturer, Paul H. Chook Department of Information Systems & Statistics, Baruch College, and Online Business Programs, CUNY School of Professional Studies, CUNY, shared his advice on assembling and augmenting OER:

> The biggest challenge was finding the best material. There really isn't an ideal resource for the Management of Information Systems course. This made it challenging and I had to be creative, designing my own slides, lessons, videos, and ways to engage the class. I also want to note that I used "free" resources that are not OER. This allowed me to have the New York Times, Wall Street Journal and YouTube videos to supplement the course. Having the ability to include some of these resources was very helpful. Understanding the difference between free-to-students and OER is an important concept.

If you are an effective teacher, being able to change to an OER text or to create a new course outline is possible. You need to be able to adjust your mindset and be creative when necessary. Be prepared to think "outside the box."

We have found that most faculty fall into the category of agnostic as far as "purity" of OER adoption is concerned as long as the content offers the "coverage" they need. Danielle S. Apfelbaum, Scholarly Communication Librarian, Farmingdale State College, State University of New York, shared how she made use of appropriate but non-OER materials while teaching an information literacy course at her previous institution:

While my course wasn't 100% OER, I used a considerable amount of material from TED Talks to introduce a significant portion of each week's topic. I was particularly drawn to the TED talks because of the ability to either read the material (each video comes with an interactive transcript) or watch the video.

Faculty are not concerned about whether they mix OER licensed content with low-cost commercial or institutionally subscribed and paid content. They also don't really care whether OER is completely open or more narrowly licensed. Their way of thinking is that if the ultimate goal is to provide high-quality learning materials at a low or zero cost to students, and if an institution is already paying for digital subscriptions, why not make use of the latter? Yuliya Zabyelina, Assistant Professor in the Political Science Department, John Jay College of Criminal Justice, CUNY, reflected this point of view:

For my graduate courses, unfortunately, I am not able to use OER but I do use zero cost materials. The library subscribes to subject specific databases that offer peer-reviewed journal articles that I use in my courses. I do not assign a textbook as I make extensive use of library subscriptions. I also prefer to assign academic articles rather than a textbook in graduate courses. Graduate students need to get accustomed to reading professional scholarly publications which offer in-depth scholarly research. Also, because my area is interdisciplinary, it is extremely hard to find a good textbook.

Even though there have been concerns and even outrage expressed over the high cost of some scholarly research publication subscriptions, many faculty believe that within reason, institutions and governments should have a financial commitment to making the highest quality and most current materials available to all students through the library. Increasing the use of digital subscriptions might also mean that the subscription is likely to be renewed, and students will benefit from the latest discoveries and trends in the industry, while instructors will be able to supplement and enrich their course learning materials. One solution to the high cost of some scholarly research publications has been for some institutions to publish the scholarship of their own faculty in open repositories or make it available for free to their institution or a consortium.

Authoring or Creating Your Own

When it comes to authoring OER, in addition to having the expertise in your subject, you will also need to develop some proficiency with technology and prepare for some heavy lifting if it is not your forte—unless perhaps you have a tech support team to assist you along the way.

There are many advantages to creating your own OER. First, you might be able to position yourself to be in complete control of all learning materials and not dependent on any institutional subscriptions that might go away with budget cuts. Second, you can create exactly what you need for your course without having to make any adjustments or compelling students to buy several texts while only using a limited portion of material in each. You can also update or modify the material as you need. Third, you might be able to further engage students with the course at a completely new level using innovative instructional methods and carefully selected learning materials. On the flip side, this can involve a lot of upkeep of materials. It may also take a considerable amount of time to just develop the content. Curtis Izen shared his experience of developing a course with OER:

> I was able to control the content and what I felt I wanted to share. This helped me build a more constructive course that wasn't pushed on students. I discovered that students found OER material more enjoyable to read and they appreciated that. My course with OER wasn't

overwhelmed with the terms and endless reading in comparison with a traditional commercial text. . . . I was confident that between my teaching methods and the material, the class was engaged.

I also used other technologies such as guided videos in my class to personalize student experiences. I modified the content and tailored the topics and course in the direction I needed. This allowed for the class to become more engaged. I was able to start each week with my own content in addition to other resources I used. Students learned about the topic in-depth and what was required of them each week.

Putting the course materials together is time-consuming. I created video lectures as well as other types of materials and added a Creative Commons license to it. I had to take quite a lot of time to find the appropriate fit for the OER text and other non-OER materials (free-to-students), while filling in the gaps with my own content.

Being passionate about teaching with technology, I spend a great deal of time learning and reading about best practices. This results in developing new skills in teaching with technology and making more effective use of OER.

As you create your own OER, consider posting it to an OER repository to share it with the world and make your content discoverable, so that it can be found and used by others. An advantage in doing so is that you will gain recognition and appreciation for your work. You may even get valuable feedback from your peers or find a collaborator to keep it up-to-date and possibly improve upon it. It can even enable you to find a community of like-minded colleagues.

Where Will My Content Live?

As you explore various hosting solutions, start with a goal in mind. Is your intention to adopt an open textbook that offers a comprehensive text, or do you imagine a collection of resources that come together in a meaningful way? In the latter case, you need to provide context for the individual pieces and possibly add prompts or guiding questions that could help your students work with the material. Whatever the choices you make, your OER will need to be easily and conveniently shared with your students.

If your goal is to replace a commercial text or to create a course only with OER or other free resources, you will need to use a platform that will enable you to host, link to and share learning materials. As you start creating and assembling your own OER or remixing OER to create a derivative work, consider the resources, support staff and technology to which you have access. Once you know the institutional resources and support systems available to you, you will be better positioned to make decisions about the OER hosting platform.

Some platforms enable one to aggregate, create, and modify, as well as publish and distribute. Other platforms enable users to engage with the works published through commenting or other collaborative tools. Some of these platforms are fee-based, while others might be free and/or require an institutional installation.

In most cases, hosting platforms are not cost-free, requiring an institutional subscription or installation as well as additional support. Some platforms are intentionally designed for OER use and have their roots in ebooks, like Pressbooks (https://pressbooks.com/). Others have their roots in a content management software and were then adapted to fit the needs of OER users. Some of these include Wordpress (https://wordpress.com/) or LibGuides (https://springshare.com/libguides/), the latter of which were originally meant to be used by librarians to curate and share information and resources. There are even publishing platforms that have been adopted specifically for OER use, like Manifold Scholarship (https://manifoldapp.org/). Furthermore, some platforms also double as OER repositories. For example, Merlot is one of the long-standing and established repositories of shareable online teaching and learning materials. Many faculty already use it to search for learning materials, but it can also be used to create one's own content. At John Jay College, CUNY, some faculty used the LibGuide platform to host their course OER. Vee Herrington, Adjunct Associate Professor and OER Librarian, John Jay College of Criminal Justice, CUNY, explained,

> *I created an OER group on the LibGuide platform and enabled authoring rights to specific faculty. I created the initial template for instructors to use. Some faculty needed a short tutorial, while others had no problem just following the LibGuide training materials I created.*

An institution might have several hosting solutions in place and allow faculty to determine the platform that best suits their needs. For example, at Baruch College, faculty have a few platforms they can use to support their creation of their zero-textbook courses like Google Sites (https://sites.google.com), LibGuides, and Blogs @Baruch (https://blogs.baruch.cuny.edu/), their own WordPress installation. Baruch College does not prescribe an OER platform to faculty, and it also has more than one LMS in place that it supports. The college invites faculty to meet with its OER coordinator, who then consults with them and helps faculty learn about the various platforms, guiding them through the different options, and connecting them with other faculty and support staff.

As you learn about your own institutionally supported platforms, you might also want to get involved in in the process of identifying and evaluating platform solutions for your institution. Visit the authors' website for a sample list of hosting platforms.

In some cases, where there is a robust structure for developing online courses, faculty might be advised to make full use of their LMS, developing and posting all learning materials directly in the LMS. Faculty authoring more extensive learning materials that constitute the equivalent of a book might prefer to use a publishing platform where they can easily manipulate original content, update, export in various formats, and simply link to it from the LMS. Additionally, some resources are best linked to, not uploaded to an LMS, particularly if there is any ambiguity about the terms of use or whether the resource has been posted with the approval of the copyright holder.

An institution might decide to partner with an OER vendor when there is an institutional strategy to support and scale-up OER. If your school uses an LMS—which most schools do these days—be sure to explore how the vendor's OER hosting solution integrates into your LMS. Consider how easy it will be for students to navigate from one platform to another, think about what platform you will use to communicate with your students and what platform will be used by students to submit their work and engage with the course, and consider how can you enable students to fully participate with course materials. When there is already an LMS in place and an institution attempts to integrate an OER platform from an external vendor, the results can be less than desirable, as is sometimes the case when it comes to any technology integration. Due to the complexity of university system configurations as well as the software itself, it might not be always possible to seamlessly integrate. James Brinson, currently Assistant Professor of Ecology at Saint Mary-of-the-Woods College, commented on his experience while at the American Military University:

> *We used IntellusLearning as the delivery system that was linked to our learning management system (LMS), Sakai, that enabled tracking and allowed me to see how much time students spent on a resource. It did not work out so well in the end, as it was very bulky, clunky, cumbersome. It would have been better if students had just downloaded a PDF that gave them that immediate ownership of learning materials rather than reading from the screen. When the content is nested into an LMS, that presents a lot more problems. It was very difficult for me to update learning materials. Due to the way IntellusLearning was set up, I did not have editing access, so if I needed to make any updates I had to go through several levels of approvals. I ended up using PDFs that I then posted to our LMS in order to have more ownership of content.*

On the other hand, if your LMS and the OER platforms are all supported by your institution, your IT department might have already thought through and resolved the issues of integration for you.

Some OER platforms might have the functionality of an LMS, enabling you to not only post content but also communicate with students, enable students to interact with content (for example, respond to a specific comment or prompt), submit assignments, and get feedback and grades. Other OER hosts enable users to download or export content in various formats. This enables students to read offline or to easily print out a copy. If it is permissible to download and use the content in your LMS, you might want to take advantage of that option. Consider how students will interact and engage with the learning materials and what their preferences might be.

Susan Ko uses several of the richly illustrated essays on Chinese and Japanese history from the MIT Visualizing Cultures project in her history courses. While this Creative Commons licensed content can be accessed by clicking through multiple branching links on MIT's website, Ko found that students sometimes lost their way navigating through each link, neglecting to cover all the assigned sections. Because the site also makes each section of the essays available as a printable PDF, providing all the text and images in a scrolling linear version, Ko posts these as readings in her LMS class site.

City University of New York's Graduate Center Academic Commons team has created course templates in their WordPress installation for faculty teaching with OER content, especially those who might not be using an LMS. Part of the process of improving those templates was to draw upon the experience of faculty who had previously used the platform to teach courses with OER. See an example of one of these teaching templates at https://teaching-template-demo.commons.gc.cuny.edu/.

Manifold is another open-source platform for scholarly publishing that has been implemented at CUNY. Krystyna Michael (2019), who supports faculty use of Manifold at CUNY's Graduate Center for Teaching and Learning, noted:

> *It allows instructors to create dynamic course materials by publishing custom editions of public domain texts and open educational resources (OER). Instructors can embed additional notes, files, images, videos and interactive content into the text to create a multimedia reading experience. Manifold also supports social reading through collaborative annotation, so students can "meet" in the margins of texts and discuss course content online.*

Paul Hebert (2019), Graduate Teaching Fellow at Queens College, CUNY, who uses Manifold, shared how he combined texts in the public domain on this publishing platform and engaged his students making use of the special features of the platform:

> *I teach an introduction to American Literature course most semesters and part of my regular preparation is a debate with myself about which editions to adopt. As a nineteenth-century specialist, most of the texts I assign are long out of copyright and widely available. . . . I experimented with creating my own teaching editions of the required texts as ebooks (.epub) and publishing them on CUNY Manifold. It proved successful well beyond my expectations because in addition to the customization that I was able to achieve, there were surprising additional benefits from the way everyone in class could collaboratively annotate the texts. . . . It also encouraged me to model good textual scholarship for students and engage*

them throughout the course in a conversation about textual variants, editorial decisions, and the circuits through which texts move . . . it felt like we shared the text and so were collaboratively building a resource. The highlighting from one student could provoke new questions from another student, for instance. In class, we could project this shared text on the board and use the annotations to jump-start discussions.

As you begin your journey with OER, it will be important to learn about institutionally supported platforms that can enable OER use. One reason to use an institutionally supported platform is that you and your students will be able to get technical assistance and support, if needed. In any case, you will want to find out what technology is already in place and how it might be able to support you in the creation, hosting, and sharing of OER content.

Replacing Ancillary Content from Publishers

Many OER textbooks do not include supplementary materials like quizzes or instructor guides or multimedia that may be supplied by publisher's sites for their textbooks. This can present a real obstacle for busy faculty who know they will need to create materials themselves, especially if their institutions will not compensate them for doing so. Even if you are not seeking to replicate such materials, in an online class, any discussions or assignments that depended on the replaced text will have to be recreated. Helen Chang, Assistant Adjunct Professor at Lehman College, CUNY, encountered some of these issues in developing her OER political science course after selecting an open textbook:

Non-OER textbooks had nicer graphics and data charts and photos, with lots of supplemental materials (like flash cards, interactive maps, simulations and exercises, interactive quizzes, reading comprehension questions, etc.). I was initially concerned about this but after reading student feedback, I came to understand that for an intro class like mine, students didn't really need all the bells and whistles. Still, while I didn't create my own OER, mostly because of time concerns, I had to update my online discussion boards and I had to create new quizzes and exams. This was quite time consuming.

Special Issues

How to properly attribute remixed content? Remixing existing content can be rather challenging. In academia, we focus on academic integrity and constantly educate our students to cite properly and use citations even when paraphrasing. It is important that we set the right example in our own work. If you plan to engage your students in the creation of OER, remember to help students understand how to properly document and cite their work. Again, you may want to revisit the original source's licensing conditions and ensure that you may make changes to the work and whether derivatives are allowed. The Community College Consortium for Open Educational Resources (CCCOER) website recommends using phrases like "Adapted from . . ." or "This work is a derivative of . . ." or "Adapted from the following sources . . ." when you have multiple sources that you combine (Attributing OER, n.d.). Whenever feasible, we think it is important to distinguish among the various entities of any remixed resources.

What if my students want a print version of the textbook? There are indications that many students still prefer a print version of the text. Therefore, you will have to think about how easy it might be for students to print online resources for your class. In some instances, the open textbook publisher will have an option to either download a PDF or will produce a print version for a low price. Consult with your print shop, your bookstore, and your IT department to explore the best options for your students.

What about access to the text after the course has ended? Consider how students will access learning materials after the end of the course. Some schools have limitations to the time given to students to continue to access the course site after the conclusion of a semester. In that case, you should remind students to save any materials they may want to retain. If you are not sure about the policy at your institution, find out what it is. You can then make appropriate recommendations to students about preserving access to learning materials.

Which Creative Commons license should I use? When remixing or creating your own content, you will want to license your work by affixing an appropriate Creative Commons license. For example, when you are reusing an OER that has a ShareAlike condition, it means that you will have to follow the same guidelines as the original when you create your OER. If you create your OER and don't indicate licensing conditions, you are not communicating how you expect others to use the content you create. If you are uncertain which license to choose, we suggest you use the Creative Commons interactive *Choose a License* feature (https://creativecommons.org/choose/).

How Do I Cite and Attribute OER?

The citation guidelines for OER are generally standardized in terms of the elements you need to include. These are listing a title and source and linking to the content you are adopting. Usually, you also need to name the creator of the content—it may be a person or an organization. The more details you can include to provide attribution to the original source, the better. The process is made easier by using the *Attribution Builder Tool* from Open Washington (www.openwa.org/open-attrib-builder/). It enables you to input information to create a proper citation for the OER. When you have one source that you are adopting or remixing, then just cite it as you would for an academic publication. When you are remixing content from several sources, attribution becomes more complicated and requires additional thought.

What About Reusing Your Own Past Work?

When you author your own OER, you might be inclined to reuse some of the publications that you created in the past, thinking that you have done all that work and it would be great to share the work with your students. It is an excellent idea, as you can share the passion and interest in your subject with your students. But do remember to check with any publishers on the terms and conditions of your reusing any of the materials that might be under their copyright. As the original author, or even more complicated, as coauthor, you might only be able to share a specific percentage of your work. If you published in an open access journal or with the Creative Commons license, you will need to examine and perhaps duplicate the licensing conditions.

If you created your content for an academic institution and it was not explicitly labeled as OER, you might want to check on the institutional intellectual property policy before beginning to repurpose it as OER. This is especially important if you created it as staff rather than as faculty, since institutions often have different policies for these different roles. There may be limitations to the types of licenses you can use or to the type of material you can create as an employee of an institution.

In Chapter 4, we will walk you through the next steps of course planning with a careful examination of each course element, accounting for the decisions you made for adopting, adapting, or authoring OER.

References

Community College Consortium for Open Educational Resources. (n.d.). *Attributing OER*. Retrieved from www.cccoer.org/attributing-oer/

Hebert, P. L. (2019). "A book that can be read": Creating and teaching with custom digital editions of historical texts. In L. Waltzer (Ed.), *Building open infrastructure at CUNY*. Retrieved from https://cuny.manifoldapp.org/projects/building-and-sustaining-infrastructure-for-open-educational-resources-and-open-pedagogy

Michael, K. (2019). Manifold for open educational resources. In L. Waltzer (Ed.), *Building open infrastructure at CUNY*. Retrieved from https://cuny.manifoldapp.org/projects/building-and-sustaining-infrastructure-for-open-educational-resources-and-open-pedagogy

Chapter 4

Plan Out Your Course with OER

Planning out a course is not a new concept to either faculty or instructional designers, who are both accustomed to developing online courses. However, online course design principles might be somewhat new to those working with OER. It's important to point out that those who teach online in particular might be more familiar with course planning tools, mainly because teaching online and building out a course in a learning management system (LMS) goes beyond developing a traditional course outline or a syllabus. Generally speaking, all the elements and structure of an online course need to be outlined or "story-boarded." When it comes to developing a course with OER, it's like lesson planning on steroids. It requires not only the knowledge of the subject at hand or details of the lesson agenda but also a profound understanding of teaching and learning and the pedagogy for online.

The Essentials and Backward Design

An experienced instructional designer or a course developer can point out the essential elements of course planning, which include but are not limited to the following: course learning outcomes and unit-specific learning objectives (what students are expected to be able to do upon course and unit completion); teaching strategies or methods (activities students will engage in to meet course outcomes and unit objectives); assessment measures (activities to demonstrate proficiency and attainment of the outlined outcomes and objectives); and last but not least—content, content, and content!

Wiggins and McTighe (1998) outline three elements of backward design: identifying the desired results, determining acceptable evidence, and planning learning experiences and instruction (that also involves selection of instructional materials). While these elements might seem intuitive and easy to follow in course planning, in fact, faculty can often benefit from the support, guidance, and feedback of an instructional designer.

Some faculty start with choosing a textbook and then plan the course around it. For example, a business school faculty member specializing in corporate finance and investment banking might simply start by selecting the best textbook she can find for her students. But after teaching for several years, she might start to question her textbook selection, as she notices that students are not performing as well on assignments as she would have expected. She then might contact an instructional designer who could help her review, refine, and revise her course. Subsequently, she discovers that she can be more deliberate, objective driven, and student centered in her course planning. She might conclude that the textbook should not drive her decisions about pedagogy. Vee Herrington, Adjunct Associate Professor and OER Librarian, John Jay College of Criminal Justice, CUNY, provided an example from instructors she worked with in Criminal Justice:

> *Instructors often cannot find the "perfect" textbook. I explain to them that there are other ways to meet course learning outcomes. You can use several chapters from one book or multiple chapters from a different book. To supplement or fill in the gaps, I also help faculty look for articles, e-books or videos. With this approach, a commercial textbook is not driving the instruction, but the learning outcomes are.*

Kim Grewe, Associate Professor of English and Instructional Technologist at Eastern Shore Community College, outlined the value added by utilizing the backward design process to support course planning with OER:

> *Instructional designers are trained to use backward design. Faculty usually know what they want students to learn. But many times, faculty look to the outcomes and objectives as they are already laid out in a textbook, instead of thinking more deeply about their own students' experiences and needs. Backward design is really a student-centered design.*

Through a process of deep analysis, which focuses on students and their learning—not just the teacher and textbook—instructional designers strive to create meaningful learning experiences. The first question to ask is what do we want students to be able to know or do after experiencing this course? How will students demonstrate that they reached the desired outcomes? How will students interact with the content? How can we guide their learning? What are we doing to help students be more active participants and less passive recipients? After we think about that, THEN we think about the content. This approach works particularly well with OER.

There are many types of course planning documents, and some institutions or units have developed their own templates. In this chapter we present an OER course planning document developed by the authors that can be downloaded from the authors' website. This planning document was first used in a two-week, asynchronous, instructor-facilitated workshop developed by the authors and discussed in Chapter 9. The document enables one to approach course planning systematically with OER in mind. You can review the accompanying course planning document (Figure 4.1). We would also like to share an example of the course planning document with one week of a hypothetical course completely filled out (Figure 4.2), demonstrating that it might be easier than you think to use this planning document. Such a template can be used during the implementation and the build-out of the course itself in the LMS or other hosting platform.

In addition to the standard course planning elements, like unit/week/module, and the learning outcomes, learning activities, and/or assignments, the sections in this document that address course content are very specific. The content-related sections guide the user through the careful review process for evaluating and selecting learning materials, examining the specific attributes of the content, as well as aligning the content with the appropriate areas of the course.

Following through each part of the document allows one to refresh, renew, or revise an existing course or build a completely new course, for which content is carefully selected and aligned with outcomes to support all learning activities. In the careful examination and planning of each individual module, one might discover that there need to be some major changes to the course structure, activities or assignments,

YOUR NAME AND NAME OF YOUR COURSE:

PROVIDE A BRIEF RATIONALE FOR SELECTING YOUR OER:

YOUR SELECTED OER (ONE OR MORE):

UNIT / WEEK / MODULE OF COURSE:

LEARNING OUTCOME(S) THAT APPLY:

LEARNING ACTIVITIES AND/OR ASSIGNMENTS THAT APPLY:

CURRENT CONTENT (IF NOT NEW COURSE): READING, RESOURCE, VIDEO, ETC.

OER REPLACING OLD CONTENT OR OER FOR NEW COURSE(IF FREE BUT NOT OER, PLEASE IDENTIFY):

OER LICENSING CONDITIONS (BE SPECIFIC):

ADOPTING AS IS OR NEEDS MODIFYING OR SUPPLEMENTING:

IF MODIFYING OR SUPPLEMENTING, WHERE WILL NEW CONTENT COME FROM:
INSTRUCTOR, ANOTHER OER, ERESERVE, ETC.

NOTES:

Zhadko, O. & Ko, S. (2017, 2019). An OER Course Planning Document: Define,
Evaluate, Select and Integrate!

Figure 4.1 OER Course Planning Document

UNIT / WEEK / MODULE OF COURSE:

LEARNING OUTCOME(S) THAT APPLY:

LEARNING ACTIVITIES AND/OR ASSIGNMENTS THAT APPLY:

CURRENT CONTENT: READING, RESOURCE, VIDEO, ETC.

OER REPLACING OLD CONTENT (IF YOU CHOOSE FREE BUT NOT OER, PLEASE IDENTIFY AS SUCH):

OER LICENSING CONDITIONS (BE SPECIFIC):

ADOPTING AS IS OR NEEDS MODIFYING OR SUPPLEMENTING:

IF MODIFYING OR SUPPLEMENTING, WHERE WILL NEW CONTENT COME FROM:
INSTRUCTOR, ANOTHER OER, ERESERVE, ETC.

NOTES:

Figure 4.1 (Continued)

YOUR NAME AND NAME OF YOUR COURSE:

Professor Maxine Weber
Introduction to Sociology

YOUR SELECTED OER (ONE OR MORE):

OpenStax Sociology Text
https://openstax.org/details/
books/introduction-sociology-2e

PROVIDE A BRIEF RATIONALE FOR SELECTING YOUR OER:

The open textbook provide content on most of the essential course topics. The book reflects the latest research and provides current examples. The text is a collective work from multiple faculty. The book has handy student and instructor supplemental resources.

UNIT / WEEK / MODULE OF COURSE:

Week 1

LEARNING OUTCOME(S) THAT APPLY:

Identify major principles of Sociology

LEARNING ACTIVITIES AND/OR ASSIGNMENTS THAT APPLY:

Group discussion and a reflective journal entry

CURRENT CONTENT (IF NOT NEW COURSE): READING, RESOURCE, VIDEO, ETC.

Jones text, chapter 1-2

OER REPLACING OLD CONTENT OR OER FOR NEW COURSE(IF FREE BUT NOT OER, PLEASE IDENTIFY):

OpenStax Sociology Text, Chapter 2

OER LICENSING CONDITIONS (BE SPECIFIC):

Attribution Non Commercial CC BY-NC

ADOPTING AS IS OR NEEDS MODIFYING OR SUPPLEMENTING:

Need to add some commentary to introduce chapter and add an article

IF MODIFYING OR SUPPLEMENTING, WHERE WILL NEW CONTENT COME FROM:
INSTRUCTOR, ANOTHER OER, ERESERVE, ETC.

Instructor to write commentary; an article XXX from an Open Journal of Society

NOTES:

Figure 4.2 Sample OER Course Planning Document

or that some new content such as instructor commentary or lectures needs to be developed.

While it might be challenging to replace all learning materials with OER for your course at once, consider starting with supplementing the existing learning materials with OER or replacing the learning materials that are the most costly for students with OER or other materials that are free or low cost to students.

Kenneth R. Weisshaar, who teaches Business Ethics at Lehman College online, has started to enhance his course with OER using an *OpenStax* textbook, and shared his experience:

> *I started by using the course planning document provided in the Lehman faculty development workshop. It was pretty straightforward and there was no difficulty. I searched the web for open textbooks and, surprisingly, found one at OpenStax called Business Ethics. I've evaluated the textbook by reading the relevant chapters and comparing them to the ones in the textbook I had used the last two semesters, and the course planning document guided me through that process. The content met my course needs, and the book had a list of reputable contributors. I'm replacing the first three chapters that introduce ethics and teach several well-known ethical theories. The biggest issue will be making sure the rest of the course is consistent in its use of these theories as foundational materials. I plan to see how it works in the course and what, if any, reactions the students have to not being able to get a hard copy of the book. At this point, I am partially integrating an open textbook into my course to determine whether to fully replace my current textbook with OER.*

Danielle S. Apfelbaum, Farmingdale State College's Scholarly Communication Librarian and OER lead at her campus, advises, "*Start with a single lesson, or start by using OER as supplementary materials. You don't have to feel pressured to go OER all at once.*"

Getting Started with the OER Course Planning Document

No matter whether faculty are working on their own or with the support of an instructional designer, course development should involve an intentional and practical step-by-step (modular) process. If you are repurposing an existing course outline, filling out this sort of blueprint should be fairly easy. However, if this is the first time you are revising an existing course with OER, take careful inventory week by week of your current/past course and note what you already have in the way of main content, such as textbook readings, instructor lectures, articles, and websites, as well as learning activities. These are the areas that will need attention, changes, and revisions for developing a course with OER.

If you teach two different courses using the same text, we do recommend that you focus on just one course at a time as you fill out the course planning document. You may choose to jot down some notes for the second course while working on the first.

If you already have a few OER or learning materials that you thought could be great candidates for your course, add those to your document first. If you did a quick search of OER for your course and came up with a few sources that look like solid choices, add them to the document under the appropriate heading. You can examine them in more detail when you review each of the modules/units of your course.

Note that you will likely not be able to complete this document in one sitting. It is best to break down your work into several sessions. It can take anywhere between 5 and 20 hours to fully complete this course planning document. For a successful experience, fill out the document to the extent you are able and include as much detail as possible. Although some elements might seem redundant or too simplistic at first sight, such as the names or topics of units/modules/weeks, these might prove very helpful later on as you might decide to change the order or adjust the pacing of the course. Once you actually begin to revise your course, you will want to create a more complete project plan, adding details such as due dates or the person responsible for a particular task (if you happen to be working with a colleague and/or have additional support).

Start with providing a brief rationale for using the OER you have selected. You might be using different OER for different reasons. For example, you may have selected an open textbook because of its high quality and its coverage of most of your topics. But you may have also chosen a podcast that is authored by an expert in the field or that covers some specialized and current topics. Or it may be that it simply fulfills the learning outcomes or is the best available OER in your discipline. Stating the rationale will help you stay focused on what this OER is intended to accomplish and will keep you on track as you spell out the details for each individual module.

For example, in Susan Ko's *East Asia in the Modern World* online history course for Lehman College, she found a good tutorial defining the concept of "modern" in the context of East Asia. However, because the website was not current, while the text and images were still available, many of the video links no longer worked. Nonetheless, the tutorial still seemed a valuable introductory resource for her students. Therefore, she decided to use the tutorial but let the students know how to maneuver around its limitations, providing the following instructions: "*Please note that many of the video resources on this site are old and may no longer be playable, but there is a transcript available for each video that you can read, and the text and images are all still accessible.*"

Define the course learning outcome(s) that apply to each week of the course—if your course is a new one and you are responsible for creating learning outcomes, you may wish to consult some guidelines on writing learning outcomes or Bloom's Taxonomy for choosing the action verbs. In a nutshell, learning outcomes are statements that describe student behavior and provide context in which that behavior takes place as well as specify how that behavior will be measured or observed. It is important that learning outcomes are learner-centered and can communicate instructor expectations for that unit/module/week. If it happens that you only have course-level outcomes, and don't actually want to compose weekly learning outcomes, you can simply note which outcomes apply in the case of each week.

Before you start carefully planning content for each unit/week/module, specify the learning activities and assignments that students will engage in—for example, a discussion, a group presentation, a quiz, etc. Consider how you will recognize that students are successful—what tasks or assignments would students be responsible for? Depending on some of the decisions you made on authoring or assembling your OER (as per Chapter 3 of this book) and how those OER materials will be delivered, you may want to add some notes to your course planning document to indicate where everything is going to be placed. For example, if you are replacing a textbook reading with some OER material, you may want to note where in the LMS that material will appear—is it going to be a part of a discussion, an assignment, or in a module content folder? For example, do you envision embedding content into an activity or the assignment itself, or will you add it as a learning resource, linked to from within the module?

As you take inventory of your existing course (unless you are developing a new course with OER), list all learning materials you currently use, including videos, podcasts, articles, etc. Now, after carefully searching for, evaluating, and selecting your content (refer to Chapter 2 for more details and for the authors' OER evaluation and selection criteria), list your selected OER content for that module.

If you choose free-to-students but not OER, please identify the content as such. It might be that you choose several resources to replace what was previously a single, non-OER resource—don't be surprised by that. What you might want to do is glance at the course learning outcomes (or the learning outcomes that pertain to that particular week) and see if the learning materials you are choosing will support and align with those. If you are lucky enough to find copious resources for the learning unit, be selective to ensure quality and to avoid overloading students.

Unless you are keeping a local copy of all OER content on your computer, it is important to record all the hyperlinks to content in your course planning document, as this will make it rather easy for you to quickly review the status of all the links and then update them within the document or within the course itself. However, you should also list the title or subject matter of the linked-to material so that if the link becomes broken, you may more easily relocate or replace it. For example, if you had a link to Keats' "Ode on a Grecian Urn" on a public domain website, and that link later became unavailable, if you had initially titled it correctly in the planning document, you would then be able to try to locate the same poem on another site.

OER Licensing Conditions

Next is to note the OER licensing conditions and to specify the licensing conditions of the selected OER. This is something that could be more complicated than expected. First and foremost, the ease of being able to identify licensing conditions for your select OER will depend on the OER type and how it is being published. If it is a resource for which the conditions of copyright or licensing are unclear, you can consult the library, or if it is on the internet, simply link to it rather than downloading or posting it.

J. Bret Maney, Assistant Professor of English at Lehman College, CUNY, commented on his initial course planning process with OER:

> *The Lehman OER faculty development workshop I took, sponsored by the Office of Online Education, provided a great opportunity to evaluate a large number of OER and find suitable substitutes for different course activities and units that still rely on a proprietary textbook. Given that I intend to draw from multiple OER, permission to adapt or remix the resources is very important to me. The extensive course planning document I created has given me an agenda and way forward as I prepare to teach this course again as a "zero textbook cost" course.*

Adopting As Is or Needs Modifying or Supplementing

Next is to decide whether you plan to adopt the selected OER (or free-to-students but not OER learning materials) as is, or whether you will modify or supplement them. One of the challenges that many OER enthusiasts face is that when they have to piece together several learning sources, the results don't necessarily form a coherent whole. You may need to provide some commentary to help students make the connections or supply the missing context. Depending on your discipline and existing OER for your course, you might be able to simply use an OER as is, especially if you are lucky to find a comprehensive, high-quality open textbook.

Consider how each content item fits into the course structure, and note areas that will need attention, changes, or revisions. Helen Chang, Adjunct Assistant Professor at Lehman College, CUNY, commented on how helpful the OER course planning document was in organizing her course revision:

> *I used the planning document provided by the online workshop and it was really helpful in seeing what exactly I was replacing with new OER sources. By doing a side by side comparison, I was able to figure out gaps in what I needed. I wanted to include a new module on media and information*

literacy, and the planning document helped me figure out where to place it. It also showed me I was missing some videos that illustrate the importance of the module's topic.

If Modifying or Supplementing, Where Will New Content Come From?

Things will get a bit more demanding when you have to piece together several resources. Thus, the last item on the course planning document is to add in the details for the planned modifications. For some, it might mean that the instructor will create additional resources, like a video or audio lecture or notes. It might also come in the form of another OER or, in some cases, non-OER resources placed on library reserve, or it might be a video offered through an institutional subscription service. Some faculty might feel strongly about creating their own content, such as lectures and slides, thinking that this is how they can best serve their students. Still others will gladly reuse or slightly modify existing resources and focus their energies on facilitating the learning process, providing feedback, and engaging with their students.

As you select OER, pay close attention to not only the licensing conditions of the resources you select but also to whether they are accessible. Though not explicitly indicated on the planning document, this consideration should be part of the OER selection process, as was indicated in Chapter 2, addressing criteria to evaluate and select OER. While accessibility and inclusive design are not new concepts in higher education, accessibility is central to the mission of openness. If you end up creating your own learning materials, remember to make them accessible to all learners. It is worth mentioning that it's not just a best practice but also conforms with the Americans with Disabilities Act (ADA) (https://adata.org/learn-about-ada), regulations with which academic institutions need to comply.

If you have the support of an instructional designer or instructional technologist with expertise in accessibility, do consult with them. They might be able to advise you on how to make content accessible to all students, so take advantage of this help and ask that person to review your work. If you are largely on your own when it comes to evaluating the accessibility of OER, simply start with looking for an accessibility statement from the OER creator—often there will be such a statement.

If the OER does not have any indications as to its accessibility, depending on the subject and the type of OER, you may want to look for the following:

- File type—Is the content provided in just one format type, or are there alternatives? Does that format enable you to access the materials easily, without major obstacles?
- Formatting—If the OER is in Word, does it use the Headings feature instead of just indicating size by picking fonts and size of fonts? Do images have alternative text and descriptors? Do videos have captions or transcripts?
- Delivery method—Can the content be accessed on any device? Does it need to have special software to use it? Is the software freely available and accessible (enables voice controls—speech-to-text, or text-to-speech, zoom), compatible with assistive devices?

In the case where you are authoring your own OER, consider these principles as well. For example, while a PDF document might be a default file format for many users, it could be the least accessible document type, depending on how it was produced. While it might sound hard to believe, the original document type, such as the Word or PowerPoint, or a simple webpage might be more accessible for some users than a PDF. However, if you initially start with a Word document that is made accessible—using proper headings, styles, tagging, and formatting—when you do convert it into a PDF, the PDF should be accessible as well.

In conclusion, after you complete an OER course planning document, you might want to share it with someone who can provide you with feedback. You can consult with an instructional designer, an OER coordinator, a librarian, a colleague, or simply anyone who might have expertise in OER (and perhaps your subject area) to serve as a sounding board. Such a person may directly assist you or just offer a different perspective on your course planning. As you seek out feedback, you might want to specify what kind of feedback you are looking for and where you could use some help, assistance or expertise. As we point out in Chapter 9, the authors use this course planning document in a faculty professional development workshop. Faculty fill it out and receive detailed feedback from workshop facilitators.

This OER course planning document is truly a blueprint for helping faculty implement OER. As you can see by the Creative Commons license on this document, you can make changes (modify and improve it!) to the document to meet your own needs or for use in a faculty development program.

Reference

Wiggins, G., & McTighe, J. (1998). Backward design. In *Understanding by design* (pp. 13–34). Alexandria, Va: Association for Supervision and Curriculum Development.

Chapter 5

Designing with Student Engagement in Mind

There is a lot that a faculty member can do to motivate and engage students with learning materials and in the learning process itself. One might argue that students should take responsibility for their own learning, and they will take that responsibility with some help and assistance from their instructor. But an instructor can pique students' curiosity and create circumstances under which students would be more inclined to engage with the learning.

Content is not in itself a course. In fact, one might say that design is what really makes a course out of content. Many OER materials are in the form of a textbook, while others may be in the form of videos or other content in "raw" form, divorced from the context of the teaching and learning experience. Even though you can upload the highest quality resources, the material does not generally teach itself. Purposeful design is what transforms mere content into a true learning experience. Since most OER are delivered online, it makes sense to incorporate what we already know about online course design into our use of OER—editing, supplementing, or otherwise maximizing the effectiveness through integration with learning activities.

What does the research say about student engagement with online learning content, OER or not? Michelle Miller asks a key question in her book, *Minds Online*: "We remember very little in the absence of focused attention. . . . How do we improve the chances that our materials will be attended to, and thus remembered?" (2016, pp. 71, 76). She lists several strategies to improve students' attention and retention of what they learn, based on "what we know about attention as well as empirical evidence on online learning" (p. 76). These strategies include building in responses to reading, through questions, discussion, and reflective writing; providing development of foundational and lower-level skills through repeated practice, including timed quizzes or unlimited attempt quizzes; and setting staggered deadlines and weekly recurring activities to space out the learning, ensuring steady engagement through frequent exposure and practice (pp. 107–110). These principles are not limited to just text. Miller notes, "in one study . . . college students viewing video lectures . . . reported less mind wandering and remembered more information when the lecture was broken into segments with brief quiz questions in between" (pp. 76–77). For example, a faculty teaching intermediate Spanish might create a video using VoiceThread (https://voicethread.com/), a multimedia tool that allows for students to make text, audio, or video comments, and ask students to respond directly to the prompts in the video, using the vocabulary from that week. In another case, a faculty might have students take a short quiz on key concepts following a podcast or a video lecture.

Another approach is a type of simple adaptive learning available in most learning management systems (LMS)—sequencing the modules of content and activity so that certain items must be completed or must be completed at a particular level of competency before the student can move on to the next module. An instructional designer could be very helpful assisting faculty in creating such learning paths, making the most of the educational technology tools to achieve each instructional unit's objectives. When attempting to engage learners with OER or non-OER content, such techniques could enable the instructor to better pinpoint and respond to each step in the learner's progress.

It's not news that reading makes up a substantial portion of student academic work. Additionally, other types of course work such as learning activities (e.g., discussion, group work), assignments (e.g., writing assignments), and assessments (e.g., tests, quizzes, exams) are often based on readings or other types of learning materials that need to be watched, listened, or reviewed.

What are some of the reasons that students don't read, or read but don't remember course content? And how can course design assist us in solving some of these problems?

Too Much or Too Complex Reading Materials

It is often challenging for an expert to estimate the amount of time it might take a novice to read, as the time it takes might vary depending on the purpose, difficulty, density, and type of reading materials.

Elizabeth Barre and Justin Esarey at Rice University have researched course workload as it pertains to course design and developed a course workload estimator (http://cte.rice.edu/workload/) that enables faculty or instructional designers to plan out a course effectively and ensure that the number and type of learning activities as well as the amount and type of course content is appropriate and adequate for the number of hours allocated. They also have done extensive research on reading rates, identifying factors that increase or decrease the amount of time spent on task. You might find such a tool rather helpful in estimating the various amounts of time that might be needed for student to accomplish different course tasks.

If you have found an OER that seems too complex for the reading level of your students, you have a few choices: you can try to find another OER; you can provide supplementary materials in the form of introductory commentary or lectures or even other OER to help students better understand it; or you can expect students will take more time to digest the content and therefore cut down the amount of weekly content or provide supplementary materials. For example, perhaps the OER you have found was intended for a graduate student audience, but it remains the only high-quality OER source that you found on a particular topic. In that case, you could still assign it to your undergraduate class but schedule more time to read it and offer guideline questions, instructor commentary, or a wrap-up summary to help explain some of the more complex concepts and unfamiliar vocabulary.

The Reading Is Rarely Used or Not Clearly Linked to Class Activity

Have you ever taken a class where your instructor barely used a textbook? This is not an uncommon experience for students. There are a few variations of that scenario. First, it may be that an instructor assigns only a few select chapters out of a large book. On one hand, students might be excited that not all 400 pages need to be read. On the other hand, students might feel frustrated that after they spent the money to buy the expensive textbook, it is not being fully used. Even in the case of an OER text which does not involve any cost and removes some of that feeling of chagrin, students might still wonder why they are being asked to read so little of the text.

Second, the instructor might assign every single chapter in the book but might not necessarily connect it to what happens in class or relate the reading back to the concepts explained in the text when lecturing. In another situation, the instructor ends up reciting everything in the text in his lectures, essentially telling student in a summary form what's already written in the text. Perhaps the instructor is trying to elucidate and provide commentary, but that is not made clear to students, and they might think they can simply avoid reading at all. Thus, an intentional approach to using course content (OER or not-OER) is an essential element of course design and can ensure that students will actually engage with the material.

More Reasons for Why Students Don't Read . . .

Clair-Thompson, Graham and Marsham (2018) list several factors that might have impact on student reading practices: expectations, perceived benefits, course structure, lack of time, practicalities, and confidence. What this really means is that some students might not come to class prepared because they were not clear about what they were supposed to read or that it was important or necessary for them to carefully read to better understand the topic or excel on the test. In another case, the course might not be organized in a way that recognizes the importance of reading. For example, an instructor of a hybrid course might continue to run the class as though it were a traditional in-person class, conducting a lecture that covers the readings and making provision for little or no follow-up in the online portion of the class. Or perhaps there are too many other course activities or too many assignments to submit, so that there is simply not enough time to do all the readings. It might also happen that the OER is difficult to access, or the portions to be read cannot easily be located, or the student has to toggle back and forth between different sites on the internet and the LMS in order to perform the requisite activities. In such a case, students might simply get frustrated and neglect to thoroughly complete the assigned readings and activities.

There may also be a generational challenge in that students are used to reading short form materials or watching videos online or communicating via social media. Jean M. Twenge, psychology professor at San Diego State University, has written several books on this topic, claiming that constant connectedness in the online space and no reading are common attributes for the new generations (2018). However, it may be that this switch to shorter attention spans and lack of sustained reading is becoming increasingly common throughout our population as a whole. While good course design may not completely eliminate this effect, it certainly can do much to alleviate it.

Some More Strategies

In addition to the instructional strategies already mentioned, how can faculty better engage students with learning materials (OER or not-OER)?

First, students need to know the role of learning materials and readings and how the content relates to the learning outcomes. It can be helpful if an instructor identifies essential and optional reading sources or puts the emphasis on the amount of reading that is expected for students to complete to be successful in the course. An instructor might also indicate the connections between different resources through specific instructions or, indirectly, through discussion questions or assignments that require students to synthesize material from multiple sources.

For example, Susan Ko provides the following instructions for week 8 in her Chinese Civilization course at Lehman College, where the discussion assignment incorporates and cannot be completed without using multiple readings and multimedia resources,

> *What are the types of imagery and emotions depicted in Li Qingzhao's poetry? What aspects of a woman's life of this period are reflected in the poems? Cite lines from the poetry and supporting evidence from the Song website, the short video on Women in the Song dynasty, and the Ebrey textbook.*

Ko also uses short, low stakes, open book, and multiple attempt quizzes to assist students with recall of the copious amount of unfamiliar facts, names, and events in East Asian history, giving students a basic foundation for assignments that involve more higher-level thinking.

After the first quiz had been completed, she made this announcement in the LMS:

> *The purpose of these short quizzes is to focus on facts and comprehension of readings so as to complement the more analytical questions asked in discussion, and to encourage deeper reading. Do go back and review the readings for questions you got wrong the first time rather than continue guessing. You should be able to achieve 100% by the third/last attempt by following this method.*

Second, an instructor can create an opportunity for students to demonstrate that they have completed the assigned readings as well as recognize good student work. For example, an instructor can ask students to facilitate a discussion, complete a quiz, or prepare individual or group presentations. Anne Rice, Assistant Professor, Africana Studies and Women's Studies at Lehman College, shared how she uses presentations to engage students with OER: "*All students give presentations that involve or add to the OER materials, sometimes remixing them in unusual ways. Students much preferred engaging with their peers through presentations. OER made creating a student-centered learning experience much easier.*"

   Third, an instructor can also help students sharpen their focus and sift through the materials to find the essential information or concepts. There are a couple of ways instructors can accomplish this. They can offer students some guiding questions before they start reading, or questions that students need to answer at the end of the reading exercise. These questions can be factual, interpretive, or evaluative in nature. Instructors may even choose one question in each category or a few questions in each of these categories. They can also have students write a paragraph or a bulleted summary of the most important facts as they perceive them. Students can be asked to bring these summaries to class (in a hybrid course) or post them in the online forum, structuring the forum so that students must post their own answers first before they can see their classmates' responses. Remember that faculty need to actually do something with those postings. They can review them and acknowledge a few of the students in class, or highlight some of the contributions through an online announcement, ensuring that each student's contribution is highlighted during the course of a semester. Anne Rice shared some strategies for engaging her students with the OER course materials:

> Students were more likely to read course materials because they had no excuse not to. Discussion board questions were designed so that students had to read most of the material to formulate a satisfactory answer. I use online materials like YouTube and music videos to draw connections to past texts. Students also have the choice to make their own videos.

Finally, let's not fall into a trap of trying to make learning too easy. We might be inclined to come in and lecture and explain to students what the text really said. We often forget that students can read!— aha, they are in college! Even though student comprehension levels might vary, most likely all students are able to understand at least a portion of the reading, if not all of it. Michelle Miller talks about the importance of providing "desirable difficulties," defined as "challenging junctures during learning . . . typical desirable difficulties include taking information presented in one form and turning it into a very different format . . . for example, synthesizing information from an online tutorial and turning it into a class wiki entry" (2016, p. 105). Providing feedback that is targeted and focused on helping students improve prevents students from feeling overwhelmed by challenges, while multiple and frequent opportunities to demonstrate their learning fosters confidence that they can meet the more challenging tasks.

As already mentioned, the way that the course is structured could become a defining factor in ensuring that assigned readings are taken seriously, such as when instructors build learning activities that are based on the readings. Effective course design can also provide opportunities for accountability. For example, instructors can have students complete a low stakes quiz based on the reading, enabling them and students themselves to identify concepts with which students might be struggling.

For a hybrid class, students can be asked to take a quiz online before coming to class or to pose a question before or after the on-campus meeting. Instructors may want to review the results of a quiz or questions and then, during the in-person class, just address the topics that students were most confused about. Another option is to create opportunities that would require knowledge of the readings—it could be an open book test or exam or a competition where groups of students would compete against each other, and the group that had the most correct answers would win and receive additional game points.

Teaching with OER in the various modalities might involve different approaches. Whereas in a face-to-face class one can enhance and reinforce the in-person sessions with additional learning materials, in the hybrid or online course, the online content and learning activities should be intertwined and mutually reinforcing. Helen Chang, Adjunct Assistant Professor at Lehman College, CUNY, taught an online class with OER, and she has also converted her face-to-face course to one using OER. She commented about the difficulties and time commitment in transforming her face-to-face class: "*The textbook replacement was easy—it wasn't too time consuming. Finding new zero cost material for the non-text material and for in-class discussions, along with visuals and activities was more time consuming.*"

The evidence of student engagement with OER may be more apparent in a hybrid or an online class than it is in a face-to-face version. Sherry Deckman, Assistant Professor, Department of Middle and High School Education, Lehman College, CUNY, commented on this phenomenon in her course:

> *I have used OER in all of these contexts—in-person, hybrid and online. The only difference I have noted is that with online, all students are required to participate. So, I get more of a sense of how each individual is processing the material than in the face-to-face setting. My online students' reaction to course materials left an impression on me. Students shared how much they appreciated certain OER materials I incorporated. For example, they loved the blog post and also seemed really moved by videos and podcasts incorporated into the class.*

For those teaching face-to-face with OER delivered online, one might organize the online course materials by utilizing an online course calendar or a syllabus to direct students to the OER in a linear fashion. For example, Jessica Wagner Webster, Digital Initiatives Librarian and Assistant Professor, Baruch College, CUNY, organizes her in-person course on digital archives in weekly modules. Using an open-source hosting platform (the university's WordPress installation), she posts her class schedule on the website open to registered students, utilizing both OER and some library materials. The library materials are accessed by students entering their credentials. Wagner Webster organizes her course webpage by putting the weekly schedule of topics and activities, including the respective in-class discussion prompts that students have to read and review before coming to each class. During class meetings, students engage in a variety of activities, which may include class-wide discussions, group-based activities, or writing assignments.

Designing a course with OER is an opportunity for faculty to improve their overall effectiveness in course design. It might be the first time that an instructor is intentionally engaged in course design, looking closely at her course, examining and outlining the essential elements and structure. While an instructor might have successfully selected an open textbook or curated a series of resources to support student learning, in order to create an effective learning experience, further involvement in the design process and the implementation of best practices in course design are necessary.

Use of OER can lead to a more careful and thoughtful course design. Transforming a course that uses a commercial textbook into one with all OER and zero-cost course materials often includes a full redesign of how the course is presented and requires knowledge of best practices in course design. As we discussed in Chapter 4, when planning out a course with OER, a faculty member engages with a course at a completely different level.

Redesigning the course to use OER challenges faculty to think about the type and kind of learning materials they need as well as the various instructional design strategies they will utilize to engage students. Additionally, when selecting each of the learning sources, a faculty member has to think intentionally and purposefully about its use in the context of the course—in effect this process is impossible to separate from that of good course design. Thus, when one embarks on the journey of teaching with OER, it must be a thoughtful and deliberate process.

References

Clair-Thompson, H. S., Graham, A., & Marsham, S. (2018). Exploring the reading practices of undergraduate students. *Education Inquiry, 9*(3), 284–298. doi:10.1 080/20004508.2017.1380487

Miller, M. (2016). *Minds online: Teaching effectively with technology.* Cambridge, MA: Harvard University Press.

Twenge, J. M. (2018). *IGen: Why today's super-connected kids are growing up less rebellious, more tolerant, less happy—And completely unprepared for adulthood (and what this means for the rest of us).* New York: Atria Books.

Part III

Teaching and Learning

Chapter 6

Teaching with OER

While some educators think that teaching with OER is no different than teaching with non-OER materials, it is important to point out the differences as well as similarities. There is a common misconception that the only thing that changes when teaching with OER is that students no longer have to pay for their textbooks, and the barrier for students to access learning materials from the first day of classes is removed. Besides reducing costs for students and accelerating their progress through college, the long-term of teaching with OER is the refreshed and renewed course structure. Greater attention to the selection, evaluation, and alignment of each learning resource results in improved pedagogy. Just as faculty must make major changes in course design when transitioning from face-to-face teaching to online teaching, they can expect to make significant changes in course design when teaching with OER.

Most experienced online educators are familiar with issues related to digital learning materials, copyright, and accessibility. They might find it somewhat easy to make the transition to using OER or zero-textbook-cost materials because they are already accustomed to searching the internet for relevant and updated learning resources to supplement their existing materials (unless they have been relying exclusively on publishers' materials). In recent years, publishers have invested heavily in the development of digital learning materials and auxiliary resources, such as slide decks, videos, simulations, worksheets, and test banks. In some cases, publishers have also offered all-inclusive, stand-alone online solutions, enabling students to complete assignments, get automatic feedback, and engage with their classmates and instructor. Some of these publisher platforms, like Pearson's MyLab

Math or MyLab Statistics, might already be familiar to faculty. Faculty whose courses are based on these resources might have become dependent on the publisher, mainly because using these resources simplifies and removes some burdens from faculty. Faculty feel that they can then focus on teaching rather than building and developing an online course. Faculty who want to transition from using publisher's materials, especially the auxiliary resources or the online "homework" platform, might have some trepidation about replacing publishers' content with OER.

There are two main aspects of instruction online: one is designing the course, and the other is teaching. While planning is important in face-to-face instruction, the necessity of planning is even more apparent in an online setting. In face-to-face teaching, it is assumed that an instructor will prepare lectures and conduct the class, while in an online setting, faculty are often expected to not only teach but also to design and develop online courses. Course planning and design is a very resource-intensive undertaking. If lucky enough to have sufficient support, an instructor may not be solely responsible for building out the course. In some cases, an instructional designer will work alongside and assist faculty in designing a course. At some institutions, the process of course design and development might be intentionally separated from teaching. In such cases, faculty or staff may be solely responsible or specifically assigned to design and develop online "master" courses that are meant to be shared, in whole or in part, with other teaching faculty. In fact, those designing and developing the course might not even teach it but perhaps are expected to coordinate and train other teaching faculty. When this type of a "master" course model is adopted, typically there is little or no room to modify course content, whether with OER or not.

Aside from modification of content when teaching with OER, what is sometimes called for is providing context for a collection of OER, especially when multiple resources have been compiled to substitute for a single commercial text. If you end up inheriting an online course or designing your own with OER, make sure that learning materials have been adequately contextualized. Courses that are assembled as a collection of materials that come from multiple sources, unlike a textbook (commercial or open), may not have built-in summaries, timelines, background information or explicit interpretation needed to help students fully comprehend the subject.

Susan Ko uses a variety of different OER and other free materials each week in her Chinese Civilization course—she provides a very brief description of each when listing the readings and resources and explains how the various sources fit together. She also tries to help students grasp the long and somewhat overwhelming history of China expressed in dynasties and centuries, not only by referring students to timelines but also to relevant comparisons. For example, she posted the following,

> *The week we look at the period which is variously referred to in our readings and resources as the Age or Era of Division, Period of Disunion, Three Kingdoms and Northern and Southern Dynasties, etc. Well, you get the picture!*

> *Another way to think of this period is that it is more than 350 years (220 AD to 589 AD) from the downfall of the Han till the unification of China under the establishment of the Sui dynasty. Think about what a long period that actually is! In New York history terms, it is about the same amount of time since the English took over from the Dutch and renamed us New York in 1664!*

> *While there is a tendency to focus on the major dynasties and their accomplishments, it also makes sense to pay close attention to what happens in these long stretches of time in which various mini-states coalesce and reconfigure what we think of as China and Chinese culture.*

In order to facilitate student learning, an instructor can build in contextual commentary, either by adding the content in the form of recorded or written lecture or by embedding it into discussions and other learning activities.

Providing feedback is yet another way to offer context, ranging from individual assignment feedback, to automatic feedback in quizzes, to summaries and observations directed to the entire class on the subtleties of a topic. While this may often be impromptu feedback, after the first time teaching the class, it is often possible to retain and repurpose such comments. For example, Susan Ko is teaching an introductory humanities class which offers a public domain translation of the Chinese poet Han Shan that contains scant background information for students with little or no experience reading literature in translation or in Chinese poetry. She typically posts the following in announce-ments or in discussion each time she teaches the course:

> *When we read a poem in translation, we should always be aware that translators have to make some choices in regard to the plain meaning of the words versus conveying a sense of the emotions, mood, style, or cultural context. Not an easy thing to do! Please read this blog arti-cle that discusses the major translations, each very different, made by scholars and English language poets of one of Han Shan's poems. Note that the different translations often reflect different ways to interpret this poem.*

If you teach a subject that is dependent on current news or events, one of the challenges is keeping up with the fast-changing nature of the subject, adding another level of complexity. Anna Matthews, an associate professor in the dental hygiene program at New York City College of Technology, addresses how the fluid nature of the subject itself makes it difficult to commit to just a single source of material (Bakaitis, 2018, para. 5):

> *Pharmacology is a study of drugs and their effects on the human body and in our Dental Hygiene course, particular emphasis is placed on the drugs and their therapeutic and adverse effects on the oral cavity. Staying current about new and emergent diseases and therapies is vital to providing safe patient care. . . . I have been and will continue to review the information for accuracy and provide periodic updates.*

Anne Rice, Assistant Professor, Africana Studies and Women's Stud-ies at Lehman College, CUNY, shared her interest in teaching with OER, while considering currency, relevance, and perspectives embed-ded in her course content,

> *I am always interested in keeping Africana Studies at the forefront of cur-riculum development. I have become much more creative in my pedagogy as a result of OER.*
>
> *OER should be treated very carefully to ensure that the learning experi-ence remains as meaningful and comprehensive as it would be with a*

traditional textbook. With the opportunity that comes with OER comes great responsibility to make sure that material does not reproduce old biases and hierarchies.

Yuliya Zabyelina, Assistant Professor in the Political Science Department at John Jay College of Criminal Justice at the CUNY, noted that the use of OER has helped transform her course,

> *Once I started to use OER in my teaching, my course become more up to date and more engaging for the students. Many of the OER materials are case studies, popular articles, they are more powerful and engaging for students. The use of OER enables me to make my course more relevant. In my field it takes two to three years for an academic article to be published, while OER resources like media resources are easily accessible and available immediately to students, and make it much easier for students to grasp complex topics.*

Faculty teaching with OER should take advantage of the access they have to a wide range of high-quality learning materials from news articles and films to academic articles and ebooks, all available through library subscriptions. Because she teaches a fully online class in which many students are not easily able to access the library's books in person, Susan Ko makes use of ebooks from the Lehman library subscription base to provide one option as the basis for a final essay in her Chinese Civilization class. She asks students to make a selection from among ten literary or historical books that she knows are easily located and fully available online. In developing the course, scouting out and thoroughly vetting the available library ebooks in Chinese history and culture was an important aspect of course preparation.

Involving students in the curation and even the creation of OER can lead to new possibilities and improved pedagogy. Miriam Deutch, Associate Professor at the Brooklyn College Library, CUNY, shared her experience working with faculty who teach with OER:

> *It is deeply gratifying to see how OER have also inspired a shift in pedagogy, especially towards an open pedagogy. More and more instructors at Brooklyn College are interested in having their students contribute to course content, or act as creators of information, rather than simply consumers of it. This approach not only engages the student with*

the world outside of the classroom, but also supports students' contribu-
tions to public knowledge and a real-world applicability of their assign-
ments. Faculty see how open pedagogy or a digital scholarship project
develops students' critical thinking, analytical skills, and information
and digital literacy—basically requiring the same research and writing
skills as a research paper. OER at Brooklyn College also help advance
other innovative pedagogies such as the flipped classroom, hybrid and
online teaching, digital pedagogy, and high-impact teaching practices.

Involving students in the curation or creation of OER has the potential to enrich the entire learning experience. See Chapter 7 for more
details on engaging students with OER.

As you transition to teaching with OER, you might be wonder-
ing what the potential benefits or downside might be as it relates to
student learning and experience. It really will depend on whether
you are simply swapping your commercial text with free materials
or making more substantial changes in your course. Helen Chang,
Adjunct Assistant Professor, Department of Political Science at
Lehman College, CUNY, shared her experience as she started to
teach her courses with OER and no longer required students to
purchase a textbook:

I know it made a difference for many students at the start of the class. Stu-
dents were falling behind less and I had 4–6 fewer withdrawals at the start
of the course. By the end, the number of withdrawals mostly evened out.
I no longer received excuses about not getting the textbook, being able to
access it, which is an indication that students were probably reading more.
More students were using the open textbook in their coursework. I require
references in written work and the OER textbook was used far more than
the traditional textbook had been in previous semesters.

Sherry Deckman, Assistant Professor, Department of Middle and
High School Education, Lehman College, CUNY, offered additional
perspective on the benefits of OER for students:

It seems to me that times are changing in terms of how younger people
(and all of us really) engage in learning new concepts and content, and
that OER is poised to address this by offering vaster perspectives and

approaches. This means better (more compelling) experiences for students than using traditional materials.

I also use a lot of videos and audio materials. The students seem to love podcasts. I think they are likelier to watch a video or listen to a podcast than read a chapter or journal article.

What surprised me is how using OER can democratize education in that the authors/creators aren't just academics. For instance, for two semesters I have used a blogpost written by a current Teachers College PhD candidate. My students love it. This past summer, a number of them said it's the best thing they've been required to read. That author's voice isn't available in fancy journals or academic books.

Bertrade Ngo-Ngijol Banoum, Chair at the Department of Africana Studies and Director of the Women's Studies Program at Lehman College, CUNY, expanded further on this point, delving into the advantages of teaching with OER:

Using OER in my two Introduction to Women's Studies and African Civilization classes has opened up new opportunities in open pedagogy, teaching and learning enhancement. I have found researching, developing and using Open Educational Resources the past two academic years very productive as they have made the learning process more dynamic and democratic. An OER in my Women's Studies class has proven to raise all voices and bring our students to the cutting edge of the ever-evolving field of feminist and women's and gender studies.

When teaching with OER you will have to commit to continuing to update and sometimes rethinking your learning materials and course activities. Updating your course might consist mainly of revising and refreshing the content of the course, but rethinking the course might result in redesigning and restructure large portions of the course. Professor Jessica Wagner Webster at Baruch College at CUNY shared her teaching journey with OER:

I teach an undergrad course on digital archives, and very few courses on that subject are geared toward undergrads—the subject is generally taught to graduate students preparing for a career in the archives field. There are really no textbooks on the subject geared toward undergraduate novices. Further, my course focuses on current events topics and how digital archives concepts can be a lens through which we can understand the world; therefore, it would be hard to find a relevant textbook that has topical and current information. So, I had to find relevant professional literature, articles in magazines and newspapers, podcasts, and book chapters in related disciplines to cobble together the content I wanted to teach, and supplement and focus the material for the students via my lectures.

As part of my course, I assigned students to do blog post responses to the readings, and they were able to choose which readings to respond to. I used their engagement with the learning material and interest level in the readings to help me decide which readings to keep when I taught the course a second time, and I was able to determine what was most relevant to the course.

No matter whether your course changes are relatively minor or extensive in nature, it is important to stay organized to keep track of the multiple resources and revisions. As we mentioned in Chapter 4, keeping a course planning document where you list and detail your OER learning materials as they relate to different aspects of your course will allow you to replace your course materials more easily. Ideally, you will have embedded all your learning materials and course activities directly into your learning management platform, while the course planning document will serve as a guide for making changes in a more efficient manner.

When teaching with OER, do not expect the OER to do all the work for you. Just because OER is delivered online does not mean it will teach students by itself. OER needs to be seen as part of the larger online course environment. Ideally, students should interact with OER in the context of the course learning activities. This can only happen with instructor mediation, moderation, and facilitation. Being intentional in your teaching and providing adequate direction will enable students to follow learning paths you have built with OER. The course planning document presented in Chapter 4 provides a draft script for the action plan in a course. Those with experience teaching online know that the role of an instructor is vitally important if students are to engage in learning that involves higher levels of thinking. Just as the online mode of instruction made educators reenvision the role of the instructor, OER-enhanced teaching can also present new and promising possibilities.

Reference

Bakaitis, E. (2018, February 27). *Interview with an OER faculty fellow (Anna Mathews)*. Retrieved from https://library.citytech.cuny.edu/blog/interview-with-an-oer-faculty-fellow/

Chapter 7

Learning with OER: Student Voices in OER

The cost of textbooks and the ease of access to materials are often foremost in students' minds when they are asked to comment about OER. Other benefits of OER might not be readily apparent to them, such as improved pedagogy and course design. As you speak to students about college experience and ask about the cost of textbooks, you might hear how students have to make painful choices about purchasing a text or paying for rent. You might also hear how resourceful they are about borrowing, copying, or finding used copies or old editions. Unfortunately, there are some students who will try to pass the course without obtaining or reading the book at all.

It might come as no surprise that one of the main reasons that students are enthusiastic about OER is that they no longer have to pay for textbooks. While students might not be familiar with the term "OER," they know free when they see it!

Anne Rice, Assistant Professor, Africana Studies and Women's Studies at Lehman College, commented on the popularity of courses for which all learning materials are free to students: "The zero textbook cost designation guarantees that my class fills up quickly, often with students who might not have otherwise considered a course in Africana Studies. Our students really appreciate the lifting of the financial burden."

Faculty are more likely to overcome challenges related to the time and effort involved in redesigning their courses with OER when they learn about the financial struggles of students and the negative consequences for their college experience of costly course materials.

Cost and Quality

Students already have high costs for degree attainment as well as other obstacles that could prevent them from being successful in college. Eliminating high textbook costs can enable students to focus on learning rather than working or borrowing money in order to pay for expensive textbooks. The *Chronicle of Higher Education* (Redden, 2011) noted that according to a survey by the U.S. Public Interest Group, 7 in 10 students didn't purchase a textbook because it was too expensive, and 60% of students had delayed purchasing textbooks until they had received their financial aid. While students may be able to use financial aid or scholarships to pay for textbooks and other learning materials, there are certain limitations that might prevent access to learning materials on the first day of class. For example, financial aid needs to be fully processed and awarded before students can use it to purchase textbooks, which does not always perfectly align with the academic calendar. Additionally, some scholarships pay only for tuition. In some instances, campus bookstores might not offer the best price available, but students may be able to rent a textbook online through a third-party provider for a fraction of the listed bookstore price. However, when faculty use a course bundle, which includes a textbook and access to an online lab or other resources, it may also limit students in their ability to locate less expensive, alternative solutions for course materials.

Faculty demonstrate that they care about students by using OER while attempting to keep high-quality standards for learning materials. Yuliya Zabyelina, Assistant Professor in the Political Science Department at John Jay College of Criminal Justice, CUNY, shared her perspective:

> *I care about my students' budget—textbooks are very expensive and life in the city is also expensive. It is challenging to find high quality OER on the subject of criminal justice or organized crime, as it is a narrow field. Quality of OER materials is one of the main obstacles to using OER. For my courses, I use reports produced by international organizations, which are not academic but are empirical . . . and work well for my students.*

Sherry Deckman, Assistant Professor, Department of Middle and High School Education at Lehman College, CUNY, shared her initial motivation to explore OER:

> *I became increasingly interested in OER because of a desire to keep course costs low for students. In the case of the OER materials I currently use, I find them to be high quality (otherwise, I wouldn't use them)—I use learning material that offers a certain perspective or special content.*

Anne Rice, Assistant Professor, Africana Studies and Women's Studies at Lehman College, CUNY, emphasized her concerns about maintaining quality: "It is important to make sure that we continue to provide quality learning, as I believe we can do with OER."

Many faculty are aware of the often prohibitive costs of textbooks, while others might not realize that it is a real concern for students. Faculty and institutions need to be more aware of the serious obstacles that the high costs of course materials present to students and engage in careful selection and evaluation of content. (See Chapter 2 for more information about selection and evaluation of OER.)

Types of OER and Access "On-the-Go"

In regard to the digital nature of learning materials, students see both the positive and the less advantageous aspects of OER as online materials. Students in Helen Chang's online political science class remarked on these both of these aspects of OER in anonymous surveys she administered to gauge their response to OER course content.

One student commented that having a textbook for the course was appreciated, but the fact that it was an online text made it much more convenient, and moreover, with it downloaded onto a smartphone, the student was able to access it on the go. However, although another student really liked that the book was free of charge, he found one of the ebook formats hard to manage, requiring multiple tries and some fumbling before finally figuring out how to download it to a mobile device.

OER might offer the often-desired flexibility and convenience for some students, enabling them to make use of their free time and study anywhere they might be. For those students who are less accustomed to an online environment, online materials might be frustrating, due to some technical difficulties they might encounter.

While text and reading have been traditionally used to support student learning, multimedia (audio, video, and graphic/visual) materials can also enhance and strengthen the student experience. Some faculty might be inclined to create their own OER learning materials, while others choose to find and adopt existing materials without making modifications. (See Chapter 3 for more information about adopting or creating your own OER.)

When teaching online, instructors often have to make use of a learning management system (LMS) and post learning materials directly into the LMS for students to work through the course. Yuliya Zabyelina, Assistant Professor in the Political Science Department at the John Jay College of Criminal Justice, CUNY, described how she provided access to course materials to her students:

> When I teach my undergraduate courses, I use the University Modules Series on Organized Crime, content that I contributed to creating for the United Nations Office on Drugs and Crime. While developing OER materials we prepared materials that are low-tech, in Word files, taking into consideration the varying levels of access learners might have. I just copy the text into my course in the LMS and repurpose some of the learning activities. I use quizzes and some of the questions for the discussion board. I also use online films and YouTube. Students should really access the course using a computer—there is really no simple way for them to download all module materials as they have to engage within the course. But they can certainly download the reading materials to access offline.

Most of the LMSs have a mobile app that enables students to access learning materials from anywhere, without having to carry a heavy backpack, and so they are able to study on the go. However, the mobile app is not always the preferred way to access course content in the LMS because there might be some learning activities that are not available or accessible via the mobile version.

For students who embrace digital learning materials, OER might offer flexibility and convenience, while others might prefer a traditional hard copy text. While some students in Helen Chang's online political science class at Lehman College reported that they preferred the ease of highlighting, underlining, and writing notations in the margins of a hard copy book, others mentioned that they simply resorted to printing out the selected pages of the text they wanted to notate and felt no need to possess the entire text in hard copy.

Bertrade Ngo-Ngijol Banoum, Chair at the Department of Africana Studies and Director of the Women's Studies Program at Lehman College, CUNY, commented on the preference of some of her students for hard copy materials:

> *Most students rate OER positively, citing accessibility and zero cost. But nearly half my students feel the need to print out their texts to be able to read and make notes efficiently. A few find it difficult to get used to the practice of having a class without a physical book but adapt as they move along and start enjoying their ease to read on their hand-held device. Overall, students really appreciate that they can all have access to their course materials from the first day of classes.*

While there are various ways to print out OER materials, making it still less expensive than purchasing a traditional text, it may be less convenient or too costly for some students, especially in the case of larger texts.

Students benefit when learning materials include more than just a traditional text, but individual students might have different preferences regarding the use of the non-text learning materials such as video or audio. Podcasts were a favorite of some students in Helen Chang's online political science class, while others preferred videos and other visual media. Still other students appreciated all kinds of media, seeing these as providing a respite from lengthy assigned readings. Thus, when planning to teach with OER, it is a good practice to utilize a variety of different types of learning materials to support learning.

Better Learning with OER

How often do you hear students say, "*I bought a textbook that we do not really use, I felt like I was just wasting my money*"? Students want to make sure that learning materials are used to support their learning—just like we all might want to ensure that we are not wasting our resources. Students do show their awareness of the role that a book can play in the entirety of their learning experience. But they may also realize that the price of a book does not always guarantee quality. One of Helen Chang's students in her online political science class made a particularly astute observation: that a book need not be expensive to be good quality, and that while a book may provide a framework for the course, in an online class in particular, the student's own level of participation, time management, and organization is likely to make a bigger difference in student success.

Careful selection of OER also enables faculty to intentionally craft a learning path and design an engaging learning experience for each student. When learning materials are organized to support student learning in weekly units, allowing students to easily access the assignments and the associated content, they remain more engaged in the learning process.

Involving Students in OER

Studies have demonstrated the importance of engaging students in the learning process because it increases their attention and focus, motivates them to study, and practice higher-order thinking skills (Donaldson & Conrad, 2013; Miller, 2016). One the most effective ways to engage students in the learning process is to incorporate authentic assignments that enable students to contribute to the body of knowledge while making progress toward their course work.

Students can be a valuable resource, assisting with OER curation, creation, and revision in a particular course or becoming OER advocates at your institution. The importance of student involvement cannot be overlooked, because students are the largest group of users that an institution is serving, and yet many of the initiatives often take place on college campuses without their input. When it comes to OER initiatives, there are plenty of opportunities to engage students and make their learning experiences even more meaningful. There have been many attempts to engage students in the process of creation of OER that have been researched and documented (Azzam et al., 2017; Murray, 2008; Randall, Johnson, West, & Wiley, 2013; Wiley, Webb, Weston, & Tonks, 2017).

You may wish to start with engaging students in the process of curating OER materials, which might be an easier lift and can immediately lead to the enhancement of your current course. Another great way to involve students is to have them assess OER. At LaGuardia

Community College, CUNY, the library launched a 14-week hybrid seminar to engage students in the process of evaluating textbooks, both OER and commercial. During the seminar, students were engaged in a range of activities including completing a survey, composing critical reviews of textbooks, writing reflective essays, and participating in focus-group discussions. The seminar intended to leverage student input in textbook selection and empower students to become OER advocates to support learning. One of the students participating in the LaGuardia OER Textbook Seminar wrote in her reflection on its webpage (Nakesha, 2018, para. 3):

> We should give evaluation on textbooks for the same reason we evaluate professors at the end of the semester. To give feedback and to understand what is working and what is not working. To help us with our competency and to prepare the next students who are planning on using the textbook.

Engaging students in the process of OER creation will require planning, course modifications, and preparing students for that activity. Loretta Brancaccio-Taras, Director of the Center for e-Learning at Kingsborough Community College (KCC), CUNY, shared how a faculty member she supported had engaged students with OER:

> One example of OER work at KCC is in the Comparative Anatomy course. The professor for this biology major elective was interested in creating a lab manual. We began by searching for images that would accompany text and experimental procedures the instructor planned on writing. After searching for open images, only a handful were identified. In order to get color, labeled images, the professor decided to have the students take photographs of their dissected specimens. Each week, student groups were assigned a particular specimen and were asked to submit labeled images. These submissions replaced course quizzes. By the end of the semester, the professor had a wide range of relevant images to select from and students were cited as the creators. This comparative anatomy lab manual is now complete and will be used in the next course offering. Students reported that they learned a lot in the process and felt that contributed to something bigger.

An instructor needs to rethink course structure, as well as activities and assignments, to effectively involve students in creating or curating OER. While working on OER-related assignments, students may develop crucial and valuable skills such as digital literacy skills, research skills, improved writing skills, and capacity to write for diverse audiences. Students may also develop collaborative skills and become more motivated and engaged.

While students might not be familiar with the term OER or realize all the implications of OER in a course, students might be very much eager to discover courses that are free of textbook costs. Some schools, having made strides in adopting OER, have also adopted a "zero-textbook cost (ZTC)" or "TXT0" attribute for courses that don't require students to purchase a textbook. The designation may also indicate that there is no cost for learning materials beyond the textbook (for example, an online lab). At CUNY, for example, students are able to search for courses across all schools in the university system using such an attribute. Faculty at the University of Hawaii can assign a "TXT0" attribute, indicating courses that are using OER or learning materials that are free to students.

Usually, the unit responsible for OER will take on the responsibility for ensuring adequate communication to inform students about OER course designations. Establishing a webpage that explains what OER are and how to search for courses with such designations could be of help to students. Since OER originated from a need to lower costs to students, it is important that students are well-informed about the existence of OER and how to find ZTC courses.

References

Azzam, A., Bresler, D., Leon, A., Maggio, L., Whitaker, E., Heilman, J., . . . McCue, J. D. (2017). Why medical schools should embrace Wikipedia: Final-year medical student contributions to Wikipedia articles for academic credit at one school. *Academic Medicine, 92*(2), 194–200. doi:10.1097/ACM.0000000000001381

Donaldson, J. A., & Conrad, R.-M. (2013). *Engaging the online learner: Activities and resources for creative instruction.* San Francisco, Calif: Jossey-Bass.

Miller, M. (2016). Minds online: Teaching effectively with technology. Cambridge, MA: Harvard University Press.

Murray, J. B. (2008). *Was introducing Wikipedia to the classroom an act of madness leading only to mayhem if not murder?* Retrieved June 10, 2019, from https://en.wikipedia.org/wiki/User:Jbmurray/Madness

Nakesha. (2018, June 17). Final OER seminar reflection. *LaGuardia Open Educational Resources (OER) Textbook Seminar.* Retrieved from https://oerseminar.commons.gc.cuny.edu/category/uncategorized/

Randall, D. L., Johnson, J. C., West, R. E., & Wiley, D. (2013). Teaching, doing and sharing project management: The development of an instructional design project management textbook. *Educational Technology, 53*(6), 24–28.

Redden, M. (2011). 7 in 10 students have skipped buying a textbook because of its cost, survey finds. *The Chronicle of Higher Education.* Retrieved from www. chronicle.com/article/7-in-10-Students-Have-Skipped/128785

Wiley, D., Webb, A., Weston, S., & Tonks, D. (2017). A preliminary exploration of the relationships between student-created OER, sustainability, and students' success. *The International Review of Research in Open and Distributed Learning, 18*(4). doi:10.19173/irrodl.v18i4.3022

Part IV

Scaling Up

Chapter 8

Support and Planning

In order for OER initiatives to be long-lasting, they require careful planning and cross-unit collaboration. Before you begin, be clear about what OER means to you and your institution. In many cases, OER work primarily focuses on cost reduction for students as a means to accelerate student progress to degree completion. While the OER content itself is free, successful OER initiatives are not without other costs. You will need to put systems and structures in place to support faculty and students using OER, and these support services incur their own costs. Meaningful use of OER requires long-term planning to produce enhanced teaching and learning, improved pedagogy, and refreshed and renewed curriculum. Long-term planning requires that institutions estimate the return on investment, tangible or intangible, as they may need to provide justifications for funding requests.

Collaboration, Collaboration, Collaboration!

Librarians bring a wealth of knowledge and expertise to the OER movement, due to their familiarity with research databases and their ability to search, evaluate, and select high-quality materials, as well as their understanding of the various intellectual property rules. Therefore, they are uniquely equipped to assist faculty and students with OER. Danielle S. Apfelbaum, Farmingdale State College's Scholarly Communication Librarian at the State University of New York, commented on her role as a librarian assisting faculty with OER: "My main role is not teaching, but supporting faculty in adopting and developing OER. As a librarian, I am familiar with copyright issues as well as the fact that most content comes with some sort of licensing agreement or exceptions."

Information technology (IT) also has an important role in supporting OER initiatives, just as they have been instrumental in assisting faculty and students with educational technology. Due to the digital nature of OER and how OER are created, hosted, and shared, IT can help support institutions as they explore and scale up OER initiatives. Sometimes this assistance simply involves basic classroom technology and equipment. Bertrade Ngo-Ngijol Banoum, Chair at the Department of Africana Studies and Director of the Women's Studies Program at Lehman College, CUNY, mentioned the special considerations for OER used in conjunction with in-person or hybrid courses, where students will still be meeting at least part of the time on campus:

> *Technology can be a major hurdle when it is not cooperating. For courses that are not fully online, it would help for instructors teaching with OER to be assigned technology-equipped classrooms/smart classrooms, so that they do not have to go through the drudgery of setting up equipment at the beginning of every class meeting, shutting it down at the end, and returning it to the IT office. This routine becomes punishing when you have to do it for every single class. Some coordination with staff in charge of classroom allocation may be worth pursuing.*

It is particularly important for IT to be involved with OER initiatives, as it will often require adoption of courseware or platform integration that could support OER creation and use.

Last but not least, teaching and learning professionals and online education units have been key in supporting faculty development and course design as institutions have striven to ensure high educational standards in online education. It is known that teaching online is resource intensive and requires careful planning, design, and development of online student learning experiences.

One goal of this book is to shed light on best practices in course design with OER. The perspective we take is based on our work in online faculty development, instructional design, and online learning, which has taught us that both online education and OER require an intensive and broad array of support, training, and preparation. In order for faculty to be successful and effective when teaching with OER, they need opportunities to be immersed in every aspect of course planning and design.

Curtis Izen is an adjunct lecturer at the Paul H. Chook Department of Information Systems & Statistics, Baruch College, and in Online Business Programs, CUNY School of Professional Studies, CUNY. He commented on the support he has received from the two schools for his work in OER:

> At the School of Professional Studies (SPS), I was approached to see if I was interested in taking a two-week online workshop about OER. The goal was to convert my course to OER. Although I really didn't know much about OER at the time, I was very interested. During the workshop we were given strategies about how to find OER material and where to look. At Baruch, I took another workshop with the Center for Teaching and Learning (CTL). This involved meetings with OER fellows from CUNY who assisted me as well. The help I received from both schools was great. These workshops not only provided a lot of useful information, but also resources that I was able to revisit well after the workshops were over. The help from both schools was wonderful and continues to be helpful. I am fortunate that I can simply go to the office at my colleges for questions that pertain to teaching, technology, and best practices with OER.

> I believe what helped me be successful in my work with OER is the continued support from administration and the department chair. OER is a serious undertaking for the department that relies heavily on adjuncts. Ideally, it would be helpful if there was a team that could work on creating an OER course with other instructors who teach the course. Currently, I am the only instructor teaching this particular CIS course using OER at Baruch College. It would be ideal if other sections came on board to discuss things that worked best, didn't work, etc.

When supporting faculty and students with OER, knowledge and expertise is needed in a mix of subjects, including content attribution and licensing, teaching and learning, course design, accessibility, and technology. Depending on the institutional context, such expertise might reside in different offices. In order to lead and support institutional OER initiatives, there needs to be clarity that such initiatives are being made a priority, and are appropriately funded. As we pointed out in other chapters, faculty should be in the forefront of OER initiatives. Their involvement, commitment, and hard work are needed to bring OER to students, while the rest of us can play a major role in supporting faculty. We will explore some faculty development models in Chapter 9.

Many institutional initiatives compete for faculty time—it is essential to communicate a message to faculty about OER, how the institution is making OER a priority, and what support services are in place to ensure faculty and student success. Ideally, institutions will want to coordinate the multiple units that might support OER initiatives and develop a common mission and goals. Understanding how OER support the institutional mission and strategic goals will help to formulate what constitutes successful implementation and enable the institution to identify when they have reached their goals.

When there are multiple units at an institution, each striving in isolation to support OER, this can be rather counterproductive and confusing to faculty. Taking a collaborative approach is far more effective in getting faculty on board and achieving the shared goals for OER. Institutional leaders should consider whether there is a vision for OER and how institutional goals could be supported with OER. There may be a varying degree of commitment in the institution, depending on the particular program or department. As a result, the institution may decide to focus only on a certain sector—for example, lower division courses or course requirements for a major—or general education. Whatever the target for implementation for OER, an institution needs to have an intentional strategy to be successful in the long-term.

A Holistic Approach and Key Elements

Just as it is necessary to plan for institutional readiness to offer online programs, institutions need to do a comprehensive check of the institutional elements that will be instrumental to the success of OER initiatives. The Faculty Advisory Committee on Teaching and Technology at the State University of New York has developed an implementation plan template (https://dspace.sunycon nect.suny.edu/handle/1951/68190) (DeFranco, McBride, Scalzo, Brown, & Pickett, 2016) that presents essential elements to consider such as the vision and mission of OER at an institution; organizational structure, decision making and leadership within an institution; best practices focusing on sustainability and continuous improvement; professional development; personnel and resources; and many more. While an institution might not be able to address each and every element, this template offers a framework to assist in efforts to establish support structures and plan for successful OER implementation.

You Are Not Alone

As institutions start planning, it is necessary to convene a taskforce to contribute to the process of OER implementation. This group will help develop and implement a plan as well as build momentum for OER by creating ambassadors and advocates across the institution. Ensuring that all the players and stakeholders are involved and that institutional leadership is on board with supporting OER can help guarantee appropriate support and resource allocation necessary for success. Remember that faculty and students are important stakeholders, and academic leaders should invite their input. It is essential that there are opportunities for all stakeholders to be at the decision-making table at appropriate points in the process.

Establishing a multi-year vision for OER implementation enables institutions to avoid setting up support structures that are short-sighted and fragmented. At many institutions, faculty remain while administrators may come and go. Funding and resources that are made available in a particular year to support a strategic OER initiative might not be available the following year, due to a change in top leadership, change of vision, or funding source. While institutions might be in a constant mode of "recalculating" for the various strategic directions they will take, aligning OER initiatives with the institutional mission and goals makes those OER initiatives more likely to survive the inevitable changes on campus.

An example of well-aligned institutional mission, funding, and strategic planning of OER initiatives is provided by the State University of New York (SUNY) and the City University of New York (CUNY). CUNY and SUNY have received recurring annual funding to support OER in order to reduce exorbitant prices of commercial textbooks. This is in perfect alignment with the institutional mission of the two systems to provide greater access to students (see New York State Executive Budget 2019).

CUNY's efforts to address the challenge of affordability is explained in a recent report:

> *At CUNY, the short-term goal of the State funds was to reduce costs for students and accelerate their progress through college, but an important secondary goal was to change the University's culture to create systems and structures that better connect curriculum and pedagogy to student learning outcomes. Of particular interest were the use of OER in high-enrollment general education courses and the creation of degree pathways with no textbook costs (Z-degrees).*
> *(New York State OER Funds CUNY Year One Report, 2018)*

Cailean Cooney, Assistant Professor and Open Educational Resources Librarian, New York City College of Technology, shared the importance of collaboration when supporting faculty: "Collaborate with everyone you can—faculty interested in learning about OER, the Centers for Teaching and Learning, the libraries. Keep the process as collaborative as possible" (New York State OER Funds CUNY Year One Report, 2018, p. 9).

While different units might be supporting OER, there still needs to be leadership to communicate OER efforts, plans, and challenges to the institutional stakeholders and decision makers. At some universities, there might be a natural leader or someone who has been appointed to drive the OER initiative. It is important for this advocate to bring all the stakeholders to the table.

It's also important to remember that each unit supporting OER brings its respective interests and expertise to these efforts. Therefore, the way that these support and approach OER implementation might vary. Centers for teaching and learning and offices of online education have a long-standing history of supporting faculty development programming. Often their staff has also been trained in faculty consultation, course design, and teaching and learning practices, making them natural leaders in course design with OER. Faculty who are exploring OER largely on their own might want to look to these offices for help and assistance in their endeavor. It is also possible for faculty to assume the role of an OER champion on their campus when such leadership is lacking, or to join a like-minded group to collaborate and advance OER efforts.

Library Support

It is important to point out the changing role of librarians and libraries. In recent years, libraries are shifting from being the repository of print books to becoming innovative spaces for learning and information literacy sources (Verma, 2015). Librarians are expanding their expertise and services by investing in professional development of their staff and by adding new roles and positions to meet the demands of an ever-changing scope of work. At Carnegie Mellon University, library services have expanded to include collaborative spaces, gaming studios, and makerspaces in addition to modernizing their physical learning spaces. Keith Webster (2017, para. 8), Dean of University Libraries and Director of Emerging and Integrative Media Initiatives, explained how librarians are expanding their expertise to be relevant in today's digital world,

> *There are two major tasks ahead for our librarians: building pathfinders and guides to the increasingly overwhelming scholarly literature (something many librarians already do tremendously well), and partnering with technologists to strengthen the discovery tools available for scholarly research.*

The Library at New York Institute of Technology (NYIT) has created Innovation Labs (http://labs.nyitlibrary.org), a place for students to explore specialized technology resources in 3D printing and design, electronics and programming, virtual reality, and multimedia production and visualization. The libraries also lend various devices for student and faculty use including laptops, cameras, iPads, virtual reality headsets, and calculators (NYIT, Labs for Every Discipline, n.d.).

It is not uncommon to find a digital research librarian, or a virtual services librarian, a technical librarian, an electronic resources librarian, or an access services librarian—the scope of services and roles in the libraries have been changing, and more digital related services are being offered. Since librarians have been serving as guides to information and assisting students in building information literacy skills, they are uniquely positioned to support OER initiatives. They have valuable expertise in copyright, fair use, reserves, and e-reserves, as well as knowledge of research databases, and a specialized skill set to search, evaluate, and assess learning materials.

Librarians work in partnership with faculty by embedding library services in courses, by becoming a guide to faculty searching for the most recent publications in the field to supplement course materials, or by offering training and support to students on how to navigate the sea of resources and how to search and evaluate them. For example, Vee Herrington, Adjunct Associate Professor and OER Librarian at the John Jay College of Criminal Justice, CUNY, highlighted her work to support the development of OER course materials as well as instructional components:

> *I worked with the coordinator for Art 101, which has many different instructors teaching the course. An Art Faculty Resource Guide was built that all the adjuncts and other instructors teaching the course as Zero-cost could use (https://guides.lib.jjay.cuny.edu/oer/FacultyART101). Using the LibGuide platform, a myriad of OER resources was created. At this site, new instructors could find model syllabi, a course description, learning outcomes, key content areas, lectures, assignments, textbooks, policies, lectures and readings for the course. It has worked very well. A new adjunct could take this guide and teach from the very first day.*

At many college campuses, OER initiatives are started as a result of library-faculty collaborations. At CUNY, for examples, the Office of Library Services (OLS) in the Office of Academic Affairs (OAA) provided the oversight and infrastructure for distributing the State's OER funds and overseeing each college's course conversions to OER. Furthermore, the Office of Library Services provides system-wide coordination, training, marketing, assessment, and accessibility review and facilitates communities of practice to support OER initiatives.

Teaching and Learning Support

Teaching and learning professionals offer support to faculty as they envision, plan, and develop their courses. Replacing a commercial text with OER requires a thoughtful and intentional course redesign. Teaching and learning consultants, instructional designers, and learning engineers are key to the success of creating impactful online learning environments. Instructional designers are instrumental in creating effective student learning experiences, working alongside a faculty member. A report from Intentional Futures (2016) noted that there are about 13,000 instructional designers in the U.S., and with the recent advances of online education, the actual number today might be even higher.

Faculty have to carefully think about each individual learning unit, plan out the content of the course, and consider how they will be engaging learners with the content. However, most faculty have not had any formal training in course planning. Many faculty are unfamiliar with instructional design principles and best practices as they pertain to teaching with OER. Therefore, it is essential that resources and instructional design support are made available at the university or department level to assist faculty with preparation to teach and design courses with OER.

Luke Waltzer (2019, para. 1, 4; Open Educational Technologist section, para. 1;), Director of the Center for Teaching and Learning at the CUNY Graduate Center, noted how teaching and learning professionals are supporting OER initiatives:

> Centers for Teaching and Learning also began to help faculty think about the pedagogical challenges and opportunities that accompanied [OER] course conversion. . . . At the CUNY Graduate Center, we've complemented this approach by thinking beyond the horizon, focusing on the cultural, intellectual, and digital infrastructure that can sustain this investment for years to come. . . . In year one of the OER grant period, the Graduate Center fielded several requests for instructional designers and educational technologists who could support OER projects across CUNY. . . . University educational technologists can sharpen a project from envisioning and planning through execution and support. They provide an informed link in the feedback loop between end users and project staff. If our goal is to sustain investments in educational technology and open pedagogy that are currently coming into the university, we need to encode those investments in the infrastructure that supports this work. Talented educational technologists can help us do just that.

Lance Eaton, in his role as an instructional designer and faculty development specialist at Brandeis University, supports OER projects and is involved in guiding faculty in the course design processes. He shared how instructional designers are positioned to be instrumental in supporting OER-enabled pedagogy:

> *Instructional designers are key players in launching and sustaining a successful OER program. Something that does not get discussed enough about OER is that it is or at least should be seen in large part as part of the Instructional Design domain. When courses are well-designed, they have an interdependent web among the objectives, the activities, and the content. We often encourage creating courses through backwards design which starts first with the objectives (what one wants students to be able to do at the end of a course), then the assessments (how the instructor knows it's been accomplished) and finally, the learning activities (the content and actions to prepare for the assessments).*

> *If one of those is changed substantially, then it should trigger a change in those other pieces. For instance, if the instructor wants to use new assessments, then they should consider whether those assignments still meet the objectives and whether the learning activities still help students to succeed with the assessments. Given that, when OER is introduced, it should signal a shift in a course's design that requires revisiting the assessments and making sure the objectives are still achievable.*

> *As instructional designers, this is a significant part of the discussion that we have with instructors pursuing OER: in what ways will this change cause ripples throughout the learning experience?*

> *Coupled with that, we also want to make sure such OER materials are accessible to students and since that is something that we do with online courses, we're a natural fit to have these discussions with instructors about their OER content. We often have the ways of conceptualizing accessibility that instructors will appreciate as well as the recommended ways of achieving accessibility with their newly found or created materials.*

Kim Grewe, Associate Professor of English and Instructional Technologist at Eastern Shore Community College, reflected on the importance of a team approach to creating learning experiences:

> *Instructional designers are natural collaborators, often working with teaching faculty, librarians, other educational technology professionals,*

and even administrators. They embody the tenet of collaboration, a cornerstone of the open movement. The team approach may not be as familiar nor as comfortable for faculty who have grown accustomed to their individual approaches to teaching a course. Instructional designers can help support faculty explore the new science of learning, engage them in new collaborations, with the goal of creating meaningful and relevant learning experiences with OER for their students.

While there is plenty of work that only you as a faculty member can do, it makes sense for you to learn about all the support systems that are in place, as well as key units and people on your campus who are tasked with assisting faculty with OER. The support systems may be in the library, office of teaching and learning or online education, information technology, or others.

If you are on the support side, responsible for assisting faculty, consider the type of services and support faculty might need and partner with other offices on campus to build robust support systems. Consider that faculty are crucial to the success of OER initiatives, and the more they know about OER, the more proficient they can become with OER, allowing your institution to ramp up and scale up OER initiatives.

It might happen that your institution does not have an OER coordinator or a go-to person for OER. However, it is highly probable that some of your colleagues teach with OER, or at least have heard of it. Academia, sometimes thought of as a solitary journey, does not have to be that way. If you make your interest in OER known to your colleagues, you might be surprised by what you find and the support you might receive.

You might also consider crossing institutional boundaries—just like you may collaborate with a colleague from another institution on a publication, you may also collaborate with a colleague on exploring OER. Additionally, when you start your OER journey and you find out that your subject is already taught at another school with OER, or there exists an interesting use case of OER in your subject, you can reach out to a colleague to ask about their experience and for advice. You might even end up finding the perfect collaborator for creating your own OER.

References

DeFranco, T., McBride, M., Scalzo, K., Brown, A., & Pickett, A. (2016). *Implementation plan template.* Retrieved from http://hdl.handle.net/1951/68190

Intentional Futures. (2016). *Instructional design in higher education.* Retrieved from https://intentionalfutures.com/insights/portfolio/instructional-design/

New York Institute of Technology (NYIT). (n.d.). *Labs for every discipline.* Retrieved July 2, 2019, from http://labs.nyitlibrary.org/

New York State Executive Budget (2019). Retrieved from https://www.budget.ny.gov/pubs/archive/fy19/exec/agencies/appropData/StateUniversityofNewYork.html

New York State OER Funds CUNY Year One Report. (2018, November). Retrieved from http://www2.cuny.edu/wp-content/uploads/sites/4/page-assets/libraries/open-educational-resources/CUNY_OER_Report_-_Web_-_Accessible.pdf

Verma, M. (2015). Changing role of library professional in digital environment: A study. *International Journal of Library Science, 13,* 96–104. Retrieved from www.researchgate.net/publication/286711197_Changing_Role_of_Library_Professinal_in_Digital_Environment_A_Study

Waltzer, L. (2019). Beyond the horizon: OER, open pedagogy, and the CUNY graduate center. In L. Waltzer (Ed.), *Building open infrastructure at CUNY.* Retrieved from https://cuny.manifoldapp.org/projects/building-and-sustaining-infrastructure-for-open-educational-resources-and-open-pedagogy

Webster, K. (2017). Reimagining the role of the library in the digital age: Changing the use of space and navigating the information landscape. *London School of Economics and Political Science.* Retrieved from https://blogs.lse.ac.uk/impactofsocialsciences/2017/02/15/reimagining-the-role-of-the-library-in-the-digital-age-changing-the-use-of-space-and-navigating-the-information-landscape/

Chapter 9

Faculty Development

Because faculty are key to successful OER initiatives, it is essential to provide faculty with the awareness, knowledge, skills, and preparation as well as the opportunities, incentives, and recognition for undertaking OER work. This must be a multi-pronged approach, simply because mastery of OER involves so many different elements.

Comprehensive faculty development is one of the most effective and efficient ways for an institution to support faculty in their work with OER and to scale up the widespread implementation of OER. While various support units and academic leaders of the institution also play important roles, the OER transformation will not succeed without the active involvement of and advocacy by faculty.

Faculty development should be multi-faceted and responsive, addressing faculty at different points in their attainment of knowledge and skills with OER. The models and formats of faculty development will vary in approach, depending on the level of faculty experience with OER, their exposure to online teaching and learning, specific institutional objectives, and the resources available. Faculty development presents a scalable and sustainable strategy for implementing OER on a course, program, institutional, or system-wide basis.

As mentioned in previous chapters, OER is not a simple replacement of a text but always involves some sort of course redesign (or design, in the case of a brand-new course). Moreover, because OER is generally delivered online, knowledge and skills in online course design and pedagogy are essential. This is the case even when the course is delivered face-to-face but the learning materials are all OER, accessed online. At the very minimum, such things as layout of the material and student access and engagement with the content involve some forethought. Anne Rice, Assistant Professor, Africana Studies and Women's Studies at Lehman College, noted the importance of a more comprehensive approach to preparing faculty to work with OER: "Those signing up to teach an OER course should at least learn about copyright and fair use but training should extend beyond this." See Chapter 4 for more information on course planning and design with OER.

While most OER initiatives support the idea of professional development to assist in the OER effort, not all are cognizant of the importance of providing knowledge of and skills in online course development as part of these programs. This is a potential blind spot in OER planning and can negatively affect efforts to enlist faculty in the most productive fashion to create high-quality courses incorporating OER.

Who is responsible for promoting and ensuring faculty are prepared to work with OER? Depending on the institutional context and available resources, OER initiatives might be championed by the office of the provost, a center for teaching and learning, an office of online education, or a library. On campuses where faculty might have a dual appointment or reassigned time, faculty themselves might take the lead to support faculty in the use of OER. See Chapter 8 for more information on support and planning for OER initiatives.

An institution or even a consortium of colleges might offer professional development opportunities for faculty who are interested or aspire to use OER in their teaching. The format of these professional opportunities might vary, ranging from informational presentations to stand-alone or recurring workshops or year-long programs and fellowships. Depending on the sponsor of the professional development opportunity, these might be open to all interested parties or might have eligibility requirements, or have specific selection criteria for participation. An institution that is targeting high-enrollment courses for conversion to OER might give priority to the faculty assigned to teach those course sections. For example, CUNY's OER "scale-up" initiative funding scheme (which was part of the NY State OER scale-up initiative) asked its campuses to give preference to high-enrollment courses (while not excluding the possibility of others) and stated that faculty wanting to adopt OER for their courses should have the explicit approval and support of their departments.

Institutions might have different incentives and various kinds of support to assist faculty with OER. The highest incentives might be reserved for creating new OER or for redesign of courses that will be designated as zero cost. Some schools take the approach of creating an incentive or grant program to support all faculty in the use of OER, whether that entails complete replacement of all materials with OER or a more limited degree of adoption. Some institutional initiatives focus as much on raising OER awareness as on professional development programming.

Incentives can include grants and fellowships, individual payments to faculty for course development or faculty development participation, release time, various forms of recognition such as awards, or leadership opportunities (to spearhead OER efforts or mentor other faculty). In some cases, additional support might be in the form of sustained partnerships for faculty with instructional designers, librarians, or an OER specialist. For example, at Farmingdale State College, SUNY, the financial incentives for faculty varied according to the type of work with OER, ranging from $250 for the evaluation of existing OER up to $2,500 for the creation of new OER (Emerging Leaders in OER Incentive, 2018). City University of New York provides yet another example, offering payment and recognition to those faculty who have developed a high-enrollment, multi-section course and who train other faculty how to teach the course using the new OER materials (CUNY OER Initiative RFP, 2019). Open Oregon Champion Awards recognize not only those who evaluate, adopt, or create content but also designate OER Leadership and Advocacy awards (Open Oregon, 2019).

James Brinson, Assistant Professor of Ecology at Saint Mary-of-the-Woods College, commented on his experience while at the American Military University:

> There were just not enough materials in my subject area. The first problem was just the lack of overall material, but the second was the quality. I quickly realized that I did not have the time to pull together all the OER materials as one course. One thing that could have been very helpful is release time to just design a course with OER materials properly. I know departments might be hesitant to give faculty release time but ultimately it will pay off in the end.

If you give faculty more time, a semester or a year to do it, they can design it properly—it's a long-term investment. Some faculty do not need more money to do it but need more time. Then you will have a better-quality product at the end. If an administrator does not have a strong background in online learning, they may not quite understand the nuances and benefits of online course development with OER.

The community colleges were leaders in striving not only for OER courses but for whole "zero-cost degrees." If the goal is a zero-cost degree, then obviously it is all those courses required for a degree and their faculty that become the focus of support and professional development. The "Achieving the Dream" grants (www.achieving thedream.org/our-services/teaching-and-learning), by a network of community colleges and their partners, provided seed money for many community colleges embarking on the "zero-cost degree" path. They offered support, consulting services, and a means to share information related to the development of OER initiatives. The Community College Consortium for Open Educational Resources, known as CCCOER, among its other activities, also supported professional development for faculty.

What do some of the faculty professional development opportunities resulting from all these initiatives look like? The examples that follow illustrate some of the varieties of faculty development possible for OER.

Extended Presentations or Workshops

In addition to stand-alone events, round-table sessions, or panels delivered at conferences or on campus, focused workshops that include some hands-on activities are a way to offer more in-depth and transformational professional development for OER. On-campus workshops can be facilitated by university staff and faculty, or they may be offered in collaboration with a consortium, outside organization, or expert.

For example, the Open Textbook Library ("a catalog of free, peer-reviewed, and openly-licensed textbooks") developed at the University of Minnesota, is willing to visit a campus to deliver an interactive session about OER and the work of the Open Textbook Library (https://open.umn.edu/opentextbooks/). Because of the nature of its work, it also invites eligible faculty (those whose institutions are members of the Open Textbook Library Network) to participate in a paid opportunity to write a short review of one of the textbooks hosted on the Open Textbook Network.

Another example of more extensive professional development programming would be a semester-long series of seminars that dive deeper into the particular elements of working with OER. Pre-conference workshops can also provide a hands-on experience for faculty as they are getting started with OER. For example, the authors of this book delivered an in-person workshop entitled "Unpack this workshop! An OER about OER!" at the 2019 Distance Teaching and Learning Conference. The in-person workshop was adapted from their online workshop (https://oerworkshop.commons.gc.cuny.edu/) discussed in the next section of this chapter.

Online Workshop Models

Online faculty development offers the advantages of flexibility, convenience, and greater reach to its potential participants. This is particularly important for busy faculty whose schedules might not otherwise allow them to join in these activities. In some instances, the facilitator or expert presenter is only available remotely, or one is more easily able to bring in other staff (such as librarians or instructional technologists) to assist. Furthermore, online workshops (because they can potentially be recorded or archived) also capture the interactions and enable faculty to revisit and review the entire experience. Online workshop facilitators can also analyze the workshop curriculum in action and evaluate the faculty response and interaction, thereby better enabling future modifications and improvements. Finally, online workshops (whether synchronous or asynchronous) can also model best practices in course design and pedagogy.

Lehman College and the School of Professional Studies at CUNY jointly developed an intensive, two-week, instructor-facilitated, fully online (asynchronous), faculty professional development workshop for OER in 2017. At Lehman College, this workshop, now entitled "Enhancing Your (Online or Hybrid) Course through the Use of Open Educational Resources" has become an important part of the college's OER initiative.

The Lehman College approach is to focus on OER as part of the course improvement process. Faculty engage in the course design process while refreshing and rethinking not just the content of the course but also their approaches to teaching and learning. In this workshop, faculty learn how to identify, find, evaluate, and implement OER in their teaching as part of a deliberately designed course plan.

A distinguishing feature of this workshop is the role of feedback. Faculty give feedback to each other as they share findings and evaluations of OER and are given feedback by the workshop facilitators on all the workshop activities as well as on their final project, a draft course design plan for OER. In the aftermath of the workshop, they may also be assigned an instructional designer to assist them with the implementation of their course plan when they build out their newly designed or redesigned course.

By exploring OER together with their colleagues and working on an implementation plan, faculty can more rapidly progress toward implementing OER. Faculty who successfully complete the workshop are compensated for their time. Participating faculty are estimated to spend an average of 10 hours on workshop activities. The workshop, itself an OER that other institutions may adopt, is described in detail at the authors' OER workshop site (https://oerworkshop.commons.gc.cuny.edu/).

Robin Kunstler, Professor Emerita in the Department of Health Sciences at Lehman College, CUNY, participated in this workshop and commented on the value of such professional development,

> *I did not really know anything about OER but was intrigued by the online workshop offering as a way to learn about OER and see what was available for my students. The support of the workshop was essential for me as I would not otherwise have known about OER or where to start or how to think about using it.*

Kenneth Weisshaar, who teaches business ethics at Lehman College online, also shared his experience in the workshop,

> *The workshop materials on OER sources and practices were extremely valuable. I felt supported by the facilitators of the online workshop. I had no idea of the quantity and variety of materials available. The workshop was very helpful in showing me how to find and use OER*

resources and got me off to a good start with planning my course with OER.

Sherry Deckman, Assistant Professor, Department of Middle and High School Education, Lehman College, CUNY, reflected on her experience in the Lehman OER workshop,

> *I had heard of OER before, but not thought too much about it. I got introduced to OER through the online workshop. Before the workshop, I really had trouble finding relevant materials. After the workshop, I had a better idea of how to do it. For example, it clarified for me how I can use Google to identify Creative Commons licensed material and narrow my search to material that is likelier to be relevant.*

> *I started to use a course planning document as part of the online workshop. I think I will return to that when I am ready and able to tackle changing my course. I just slot OER materials in, based on a course design I've been using for some time now. In that case, I'm mostly looking to replace and update materials I have been using. I think it will just take a lot more work to replace a whole textbook, even though that is my intention. Now, I just need the time. The only support I've availed myself of for OER has been the online workshop. It was really helpful.*

In summary, the faculty development approach described here is focused on the process of exploring, evaluating, and selecting resources, with faculty sharing ideas and observations with their peers and workshop facilitators providing feedback at all stages, including the final project plan, in which they work with a course planning document. The final project plan is a jumping-off point for further course development and/or the involvement of instructional designers.

Additionally, the workshop itself becomes an opportunity for some first-hand exposure to online learning and online course design. (At Lehman, those faculty who are going on to teach their newly designed course as an online or hybrid course will further develop their knowledge during the Preparation for Teaching Online training that is expected for all those teaching online.)

Another example of an online and facilitated workshop was developed by Open Washington Open Educational Resources Network titled OER 101: How to Use Open Educational Resources (https://sbctc.instructure.com/courses/1530850). This two-week training is also an OER licensed under the Creative Commons. The workshop prepares faculty and staff who are new to OER to develop familiarity with OER and gain some experience with putting these concepts into application. Workshop participants are expected to spend approximately 10 hours, but time spent by individual faculty might vary, depending on prior knowledge.

Integrating OER training into an existing professional development training course is yet another approach. Andrea Henne, Dean of the San Diego Community College District's Online and Distributed Learning, discussed how OER professional development was incorporated into the required training for preparation for teaching online. The overall preparation consists of ten training modules, two of which are dedicated to OER, all delivered via their learning management platform. As part of their work in the OER modules, faculty contribute to a wiki, describing free web resources in their subject areas. Then faculty search repositories and discipline-specific OER sites and engage in a discussion activity, reporting on their findings. They reflect on their selections and plans to use OER in their teaching. During this workshop, faculty build a learning community and rely on each other when searching for OER. Use of OER is very subject and course specific, and even though workshop participants are able to move at their own pace, they receive individualized feedback from workshop facilitators and other workshop participants. Because faculty are engaged in reviewing OER and sharing their experiences, many eventually decide to license what they create as OER. San Diego Community College District faculty are required to complete this training in order to receive a teaching assignment of an online course (Henne, Makevich, & West, 2012).

State University of New York's OPEN SUNY has created a rich collection of online tutorials called the "OER Community Course Experience (https://innovate.suny.edu/sunyoercommunitycourse/)," covering OER related topics in a comprehensive way. These tutorials can be explored on one's own, but since they are licensed as OER, they can also be offered as part of a faculty development activity on your own campus. The OER Community Course Experience includes many useful materials such as worksheets, discussion prompts, and links to other informational resources. Phylise Banner, a learning experience designer and consultant and co-creator, along with Mike Daly, of the SUNY OER Community Courses, explained the concept and the OER approach to developing these modules:

> *The SUNY OER Community Courses is a perfect example of a project involving every phase of the learning experience design process—discovery, design, development, and technology integration. I was able to find existing OER, work with contributing authors and faculty to augment that content, and design a rich, accessible, open learning space and community of practice.*

Mixed or Distributed Model

Many campuses combine a number of resources and types of programming to support faculty development with OER. Bertrade Ngo-Ngijol Banoum, Chair, Department of Africana Studies/Director, Women's Studies Program at Lehman College, CUNY, commented on the role played by two types of professional development programs she participated in at Lehman:

> *In June 2017, I successfully completed an online workshop titled Enhancing Your Course with Open Educational Resources (OER), convened by the Office of Online Education, and facilitated by Dr. Olena Zhadko and Dr. Susan Ko. The two-week long intensive workshop equipped me with knowledge and skills to search, identify, evaluate and integrate OER materials in my course contents. Soon after, I applied for and obtained a CUNY Scale-Up-Initiative grant to develop my first OER course, during which I consulted with the Lehman librarians, especially when it concerned unclear licensing attributions.*

Loretta Brancaccio-Taras, Director of the Center for e-Learning at Kingsborough Community College (KCC), CUNY, described how different elements of professional development work together on her campus:

> *At KCC, the OER project is housed in the Center for e-Learning (KCeL). Through the CUNY OER campus grant, KCeL has hired*

> *a college laboratory technician (CLT) to assist faculty with their OER work. The specialist has worked with faculty to review their materials for accessibility compliance and show them how to create accessible documents and alt text images. KCeL has run workshops on introduction to OERs, universal design, and creative commons licensing. In addition, we had a faculty team attend an Achieving the Dream OER workshop hosted by CUNY as well as present at the Open Ed Conference.*

Alison Lehr Samuels, Director at the Center for Teaching and Learning and Lecturer at the Department of Management, Baruch College, CUNY, described a multi-pronged effort at Baruch College, using available funding to support professional development of diverse types:

> *The CTL (Center for Teaching and Learning) ran two faculty seminars that provided information on OER/ZTC (zero textbook cost), copyright issues and creative commons licensing. The workshops encouraged adoption of OER/zero cost materials while sharing best practices for implementing them in the classrooms. Faculty then had a chance to explore how they might create a ZTC course. Some Baruch faculty have chosen to create their own OER. An example of such a project during this academic year was the creation of a new curriculum for English as an Additional Language (EAL) learners in the first-year writing courses. We also continued to provide support to faculty as they worked with previously created or adopted OER and zero cost materials in their courses. This included supporting refinements and corrections of an online lab manual for Principles of Genetics (BIO 3105), as well as facilitating a peer review process for materials created by Communication Studies faculty for Speech Communication (COM 1010).*
>
> *Finally, the grant also funded the ongoing development of our TeachOER repository (http://teachoer.org) as a showcase for OER that models how Baruch faculty are using OER in their courses. All work created is openly licensed under Creative Commons.*

Librarians often serve as the lead OER coordinator on a campus and, in that capacity, may be involved in faculty professional development for OER as well. Danielle S. Apfelbaum, Farmingdale State College's

Scholarly Communication Librarian, explained the multiple areas of her involvement,

> As the OER Lead for Farmingdale State College, I provide support for faculty in adopting and creating OER. I created two incentive programs based upon the funding we have received from New York State. I also created and chair the Open Education and Open Scholarship Advisory Committee, divided into three subcommittees to educate and involve faculty in Open advocacy across campus. Additionally, I provide one workshop each semester in OER resources (recording it for those unable to attend in person), and provide one-on-one consultations by request.

Fellowship or Faculty Grant Programs

These programs generally provide support and/or release time to a faculty member. These may be just one component of a broader initiative and may also include more structured faculty development or simply involve other types of consultations and support.

Anna Matthews, Associate Professor in the Dental Hygiene program at City Tech at CUNY, developed a course on oral pharmacology with OER and shared her experience participating in the OER Faculty Fellows Program at City Tech and how the program has prepared her to integrate OER into her teaching (Bakaitis, 2018, para. 5):

> I appreciate the opportunity to have participated in the OER Fellowship. . . . This experience was definitely beneficial to me as an educator, but it also helped me as a researcher and writer by providing the invaluable knowledge on the open resources, authorship rights, Creative Commons licensing and appropriate citations, and especially permissions to re-use media (videos, images) in creative works.

Helen Chang, Adjunct Assistant Professor at Lehman College, CUNY, not only participated in the Lehman OER faculty workshop described earlier but was also the recipient of a Scale-Up Initiative OER development grant from the Lehman library, of which she recounts, *It helped me secure time and resources for creating a zero-cost course. Once I received the grant, the OER librarian at Lehman checked in on me during the semester and shared programs, lectures, and new resources via an email list.*

Anne Rice, Assistant Professor, Africana Studies and Women's Studies at Lehman College, commented on the benefits of a fellowship:

> My participation in the fellowship was crucial for success in developing OER. Library faculty have been invaluable resources for course development. The library offered invaluable support including checking for permissible use and helping to organize the format of the syllabus for greater ease of use when publishing to the CUNY Academic Commons platform. The fellowship also provided support through various forums where I presented my syllabus and showcased selected exercises, allowing me to receive useful input from my colleagues at my college and throughout the university system.

For some faculty, receiving a grant may make the difference between engaging with OER or not. Yuri Gorohovich, Associate Professor at the Department of Earth, Environmental, and Geospatial Sciences at Lehman College, CUNY, commented on this issue,

> I was curious about OER before but monetary compensation for my time played an important role. I was finally able to start due to the grant provided to faculty to develop OER. I ended up developing OER for the Data Acquisition Geographic Information Systems course, as well as for the graduate version of the course. Our librarian who deals with OER was tremendously helpful in finding materials and giving advice on OER content.

Sherry Deckman, Assistant Professor, Department of Middle and High School Education, Lehman College, CUNY, further pointed out the importance that grant and/or release time may play in contributing to faculty decisions, "*A grant provides time in the sense that it's compensated, freeing up other time I might work on OER outside of my regular work responsibilities. A course release to work on OER would be just as or even more valuable to me.*"

Assessing Faculty Development Programs for OER

It is essential to assess your programs, and often, a report is expected or required by administrators or funding agencies for OER initiatives.

It is also just a good practice to at least review what you have done and to make changes needed, based on data and analysis. For example, Alison Lehr Samuels described a three-part approach to assessing faculty development programming related to OER at Baruch College:

> *Our ongoing assessment was comprised of faculty focus groups and interviews, analysis of syllabi from courses designated as zero cost, and online student surveys. Begun in Fall 2017, this process continues to provide valuable insights, and we have begun sharing our findings with faculty through end-of-semester reports for those participating in the OER Initiative.*

Faculty engaged in faculty development initiatives such as grants or fellowships may also contribute to the assessment efforts by writing a reflective report or sharing their experiences, successes, and observations about students learning with OER. Such reports, if appropriate, can also be shared with other faculty or the university at large, contributing to the faculty development cycle.

If the goal is to develop a course with a zero-cost designation, then part of the assessment will involve how many of the faculty development participants went on to launch such a course and the evaluation of the quality of OER course content, or some aspects of the student experience. If the goal is to simply raise awareness of OER, then instruments such as surveys might sufficiently capture the effectiveness of the efforts. If the goal is to refresh and renew a course by enhancing it with OER materials, which might not necessarily lead to a zero-cost designation but might reduce the overall cost and improve the quality of instruction, then the assessment should focus on improved course design and student learning.

While there is no one right way to do faculty professional development for OER, because OER are generally delivered online, faculty development programs should ideally include the following elements of online delivery, whether as part of a workshop or distributed among a variety of professional development activities and resources:

- Basic understanding of use of the selected digital platform for delivering OER content
- Online design related to clear and consistent layout, templates, and ease of navigation in the platform

- Basic pedagogical principles of online teaching and learning for all OER delivered as part of an online or hybrid course, including how to integrate face to face and online activity, formulate discussion prompts, create online presence and community, gauge the time needed and pacing for online activities, and related issues
- Online design principles related to course design planning and development, including alignment of outcomes and learning activities

No matter what stage of the OER initiative, faculty development will help the institution accelerate, expand, and improve the quality of teaching and learning with OER. Faculty development programming is a solid investment in ensuring the scalability and sustainability of OER initiatives.

References

Bakaitis, E. (2018, February 27). *Interview with an OER faculty fellow (Anna Mathews)*. Retrieved from https://library.citytech.cuny.edu/blog/interview-with-an-oer-faculty-fellow/

CUNY Open Educational Resources (OER) Initiative: Request for Proposals (RFP). (2019). Retrieved from http://www1.cuny.edu/sites/cunyufs/wp-content/uploads/sites/48/2018/05/OAA_OER_RFP_2019_Final_R.pdf

Emerging Leaders in Open Educational Resources Incentive. (2018). Retrieved from www.farmingdale.edu/library/pdf/eloincentive2018.pdf

Henne, A., Makevich, J., & West, Q. (2012, October 9). *OER faculty development: Three successful models webinar*. Retrieved from www.cccoer.org/webinar/october-9-oer-faculty-development-three-successful-models/

Open Oregon. (2019). *2019 OER champion awards*. Retrieved from https://openoregon.org/2019champions/

Chapter 10

Challenges and Possible Solutions

When it comes to challenges of OER, we could probably write another book on just this topic. On a positive note, with the right approach, one can turn these challenges into opportunities. Some barriers are at an institutional level and could prevent a wider adoption of OER but, if addressed, could help ensure a successful and scalable OER implementation. When a support structure for faculty is put in place institution-wide, it can instill confidence in individual faculty who might be interested in exploring OER and encourage persistence in all stages of OER implementation beyond just searching for some new OER course content. Thus, by removing barriers at the institutional level, it can potentially have a positive impact on the ability for an institution to scale up the use of OER. In the case of OER adoption by individual faculty, discovering what might be the barriers for individual faculty will enable institutions to recognize what's needed and address any obstacles one by one. Recognizing the nature of institutional impediments to OER adoption also enable institutions to prepare for building capacity and increasing OER use.

If your institution is just beginning an OER initiative and might have limited resources, don't be discouraged. Think creatively about leveraging existing expertise and resources on your campus and beyond, through consortia or professional organizations of which your campus might be a member. If you have limited funding, be more targeted and strategic in your approach. Consider incentivizing your existing staff and/or faculty to take a leadership role, or bring in someone on a temporary basis who is tasked with specific OER initiatives.

Raising Awareness

Familiarity with OER in U.S. higher education continues to grow, with nearly 50% of faculty now reporting an awareness of OER, according to a recent study (Seaman & Seaman, 2018). While this is a major improvement compared to previous years, the lack of awareness among the remaining 50% of faculty surveyed still poses a major obstacle to fulfilling the potential of OER. Recently, the OER phenomenon has received heightened attention and major investments and support from federal and local governments as well as other agencies. But many OER awareness campaigns have focused primarily on cost savings, garnering media coverage and interest among academic leadership interested in addressing afford-ability, one of the major challenges higher education institutions are currently facing.

Research has demonstrated other benefits of using OER, such as increased student engagement, faculty ownership, and greater control over learning materials, as well as improved learning outcomes and new forms of pedagogy. Raising awareness about OER involves intro-ducing the definitions and the basics of OER and educating about the potential benefits. The urgency to raise awareness lies in the need to spread the adoption of OER and to scale up effectively and pur-posefully. When there is a greater understanding of the value of OER, there is often increased buy-in and follow through by all institutional stakeholders.

In developing a strategy to raise awareness about OER, one must remember to widen the approach to advocate among all relevant groups while building partnerships and involving key constituencies. Some of these awareness campaigns can be delivered even with lim-ited resources, while others would require an army of enthusiasts to carefully plan and coordinate.

One of the approaches an institution can take is to start by develop-ing an online presence through an OER website that would create a permanent, easy-to-update digital footprint for all things OER at the campus. Another way to raise awareness is to create an OER award and recognition program, acknowledging those who have dedicated their time to advancing OER and demonstrating to the community at large the value the institution sees in OER. OER-tagging or zero-textbook-cost designations in student course registration systems make it easier for institutions to keep track of the numbers of OER or zero-textbook-cost courses and course sections. Raising awareness is not an easy task as it requires planning, intentionality, and follow through.

Multiple Expertise—Collaborative Efforts

As we pointed out in Chapter 8, successful implementation of OER requires strategic planning as well as drawing on multiple sources of expertise that may reside in various units across an institution. It is essential that units that support OER work together collaboratively and in unison to assist faculty and students. When units currently supporting or those who could potentially support OER are not in the same division, ensuring that they complement each other's work rather than compete is essential to the success of OER initiatives. If you are taking the lead for coordinating OER initiatives, consider doing a preliminary review of existing resources and expertise, as well as learning what has been done in the past, to ensure that you are not duplicating efforts.

Before deciding that you need to seek outside expertise, consider leveraging existing expertise or developing internal resources. By developing internal resources, you are also making more of your institution feel invested in the OER efforts. Having a unified effort at the campus can ensure long-lasting success, as faculty and staff know where to turn in their efforts to advance their OER use. Focusing on a shared goal and keeping an open mind will help an institution to come together and advance its mission and goals for OER.

Where should one look for logical allies in the OER initiative?

The library can provide broad expertise in addition to its ongoing consultations with individual faculty. The librarians can enable faculty to move beyond the initial stages of finding and evaluating OER for their courses more quickly, inspiring confidence in faculty to undertake course revisions.

The online education, instructional design, and instructional technology staff can advise and assist on selecting the appropriate platforms and tools for hosting OER, work one-on-one to help faculty in planning and mapping out their courses with OER and with design, integration, and coherent assemblage of content. This enables a more rapid ramping up of the OER institutional effort.

Registrars and student services, as well as communication and marketing units, also have a role to play in making sure that OER courses are searchable, that students understand a zero-cost course designation, and that the subsequent savings to students from the use of OER are widely made known.

Another step that an institution can take is to join a consortium or organization of others engaged in OER implementation—this might be on the statewide level or through a national or international organization. This allows for mutual support, the dissemination of information, and pooling of resources, and through periodic communication and networking, it can foster the formation of possible collaborators to create OER as well.

Faculty Buy-In

The term itself—"faculty buy-in"—might seem controversial to some readers, so we would like to clarify it here. In this context we are referring to faculty taking the initiative to work with OER, setting the priorities, being the arbiters of quality, and advocating for student learning and the affordability of education.

Historically, institutions recognize scholarship in the discipline for the purposes of tenure and promotion and ensure academic freedom, even as institutional priorities may shift. Depending on faculty rank and faculty status (part-time or full-time), as well as intrinsic and extrinsic factors, institutions might consider various approaches to getting faculty buy-in for OER. For example, full professors with tenure might appreciate having time to dedicate to projects of their own interest. But Bertrade Ngo-Ngijol Banoum, Chair at the Department of Africana Studies and Director of the Women's Studies Program at Lehman College, CUNY, addressed the concerns of those who are not yet tenured:

> I have spent the last couple of years researching, curating and creating open access materials for my classes and hope the substantive results of my work can be taken into consideration for my promotion. This was not at all a consideration when I embarked on this project, but as I delved deeper and deeper into it and invested much time doing the work, I started wondering why OER would not be considered for tenure and promotion processes.

Sherry Deckman, Assistant Professor, Department of Middle and High School Education, Lehman College, CUNY, expressed the need for institutional recognition to advance OER use:

> *I do not believe my work with OER will/would be recognized beyond being acknowledged as continuous improvement of teaching, unless I were to write and publish about it. So, this dissuades me from investing the time I need into converting my one course that still uses a traditional textbook into a zero textbook cost course. At this point in my career, if I'm spending a considerable amount of time creating, it needs to be focused on peer-reviewed publishing, given tenure requirements.*

A focus on helping tenured faculty understand the value of OER is important, as these faculty might become advocates for OER, influencing others to explore the potential. Institutions should consider creating a variety of incentives to get these faculty and others on board with OER. Incentives could include stipends or course release, or awards that bring visibility and recognition. Faculty might also be inclined to dedicate time to adopting OER because of cost savings for students or because of their ability to create personalized learning experiences for their students that are not prescribed by a textbook. See Chapter 9 for more information and examples of incentives for faculty.

Because the need for high-quality OER is still so great, it also makes sense to appeal to faculty to contribute to their field by creating OER on their own or in collaboration with others at their institution or at other institutions. J. Bret Maney, Assistant Professor of English at Lehman College, CUNY, noted the need for more high-quality OER:

> *In my field, I find that OER struggle to match the editorial standards of traditional textbooks. (Indeed, perhaps it would be surprising if an OER American Literature textbook created by a couple of professors in their spare time could match the quality and rigor, for example, of the Norton Anthology of American Literature, currently in its 9th edition, in evolution since 1979, and benefiting from large budgets as well as a cadre of professors, consultants, editors, copyeditors, graphic designers, et al.) And yet, when resources are invested, and there is continuity, really high quality OER can be produced, such as with The American Yawp (www. americanyawp.com/) or a recent public humanities project I had a chance*

to collaborate on, The Encyclopedia of Greater Philadelphia (https://philadelphiaencyclopedia.org/). These types of carefully conceived and well-managed OER projects are to my mind a public good.

Danielle S. Apfelbaum, Farmingdale State College's Scholarly Communication Librarian, further addressed the issue of lack of OER in certain disciplines and the need for more faculty involvement:

The primary difficulty is the lack of resources in certain areas. Some of my most enthusiastic, pro-OER faculty are those for whom little OER is currently available; this includes aviation, dental hygiene, upper level nursing courses, etc. If faculty are in a discipline in which there are little OER, they should think about how they can create the resources they need. They might even want to contact their professional and academic society or association. I think if more people insisted that their dues went to the creation of OERs in their discipline, there would be a lot more options for instructors.

To encourage faculty, there must be adequate compensation and reward strategies in place, including recognition for authorship of such works as part of the tenure process (for those on the tenure track). Other types of recognition are also necessary—awards, publicizing such authorship and the resulting works, encouraging faculty to present, and supporting their travel to OER events, etc.

Finally, a note of caution: Don't oversell OER to faculty. While it is essential to stimulate enthusiasm for OER, faculty attitudes to OER are both pragmatic and idealistic. They weigh time and value for each change they make in their courses and in their teaching methods and consider themselves expert evaluators of the quality and relative importance of content in their own subject matter. The best faculty do not want to feel they must "settle for" second best for their students. Thus, in stimulating interest in OER, do NOT tell faculty the following canards that we have heard expressed from well-meaning OER advocates:

- Finding and selecting: It's quick and easy to find high-quality and useful OER. (*Sometimes, but more often not.*)
- Course development with OER: You simply replace your existing content with the OER. (*No, you generally cannot just swap out content, but must integrate the new OER into your course, which is not always simple and likely involves some supplementary work from you.*)

- Helping students: OER is the best way to ensure affordable college for all students. (*It is one great way to contribute to that effort, but so are more state and federal student grants and support to public institutions, and generous scholarships, low tuition, textbook grants, and library subscriptions to more ebooks and full text articles.*)
- Information should be free: Faculty don't earn anything from publishing, anyway, so they should be happy to create OER instead; there's great OER to replace any existing textbook or course materials; gatekeeper publishers and journals don't add anything of value, (*This series of arguments can seem to devalue faculty who do publish, and these are some of the very people who have experience authoring content whom you should encourage to create OER. It also seems to devalue existing peer review channels; and it may seem to negate faculty expertise in evaluating content or faculty appreciation for some of the ancillary and supplementary content created by publishers.*)
- Career rewards: The recognition and glory you will derive is more than sufficient reward for the time expended in creating, modifying, and assembling OER and in redesign and redevelopment of your course. (*This argument assumes that most faculty are subsidized by their full-time, tenured positions, but it is a particularly hollow pitch for adjunct faculty, who constitute the majority of faculty in the U.S. and who often are not adequately compensated even for their basic teaching duties.*)

Finally, in advocating for OER, while it's wise to emphasize that the end goal is zero cost for students, be aware that what most faculty care about is lessening or eliminating the cost of materials for students, but they are less committed to the idea that it can only be accomplished by using 100% OER content. In short, as we have noted before, most faculty are not OER purists. They are persuaded by the practical benefits and opportunities presented by OER and by appeals to the goals of providing an affordable, accessible, and higher quality learning experience to their students.

Scaling Up

An intentional institutional strategy, along with cross-division collaborations with coordinated efforts that offer a comprehensive approach of services and support to scale up OER, can go a long way toward widespread adoption and success of OER initiatives.

When developing a strategic plan or devising scale-up efforts for OER, institutions should focus on developing a 360-degree strategy.

They can start with creating an awareness campaign, then plan for faculty development initiatives that would enable faculty to learn about OER, establish training and support that would prepare faculty to find, evaluate, and select OER, and enable them to redesign their courses with OER. When planning strategically for OER scale up, one must ensure that it will work for busy faculty, as that will mean that they are more likely to follow through and be successful.

While meeting individual faculty needs as they adopt and author OER is important, just working with individual faculty to engage them with OER might not be the most effective strategy to scale up. A faculty development effort such as that described in Chapter 9 can accelerate the rate of adoption by providing an intensive workshop experience in which a group of faculty can assist each other, in addition to being supported by instructional design and other faculty development and training staff. Group training efforts followed by individual assistance has proved to be a successful model for online teaching and online course design—OER adoption can easily follow this model.

Academic departments can provide a coterie of early adopters and identify key courses where the impact of zero cost will be most immediately felt, or where the cost for course materials can be reduced, if not completely eliminated. Academic departments may already have a practice of making decisions as a unit about textbooks for multiple section courses. They might find it equally effective to use this same approach to allow faculty to identify the best OER for a course or a subset of courses, or to recommend discrete OER modules and resources that might be of interest to incorporate in a large group of courses in the discipline.

Faculty might have limited time to dedicate to the large task of refreshing, renewing, and possibly completely overhauling their course with OER, due to competing priorities. Faculty already know that course design or even redesign requires a lot of time and effort. Finding time to rework their course to implement OER and completely replace a commercial text might not be easily accomplished.

Depending on the subject, faculty might have to search multiple repositories, piece multiple sources together, and possibly develop their own content to fill in the gaps. The lack of a centralized system to facilitate the search for OER remains a major challenge to widespread adoption of OER. Faculty, as well as others supporting OER, spend hours of time looking for high-quality materials across dozens of repositories. Recently there have been major developments and improvement of OER repositories, including the expansion of features of existing repositories, such as tagging, and the diversification of OER materials, which makes it easier and more efficient to conduct a search, as noted in Chapter 2. Still, the effort needed to search for and evaluate OER remains a resource intensive task, according to a recent study (Seaman & Seaman, 2018).

Faculty will also have to consider accessibility of learning materials, as well as which OER platform to use, as noted in earlier chapters, all of which will add up in terms of the time commitment. Depending on availability of institutional resources, the burden might be lessened if faculty are supported by librarians, instructional designers, and educational technologists who can offer their expertise and assistance.

Many publishers are also responding to market demands, recognizing the need to lower the cost of textbooks. They are creating the ability for institutions to address the issue of affordability to some degree by offering low-cost digital textbook bundles for which an institution can contract to pay per student or via a flat-fee subscription model with unlimited access. In some cases, beyond offering a textbook with ancillary materials, publishers might offer fully developed online courses or even full programs. Publishers claim that this approach enables faculty to adopt "turnkey" courses without having to invest precious time to search, evaluate, and curate learning materials. They also emphasize the value added by the editorial support for the content as well as additional supplementary materials like lecture slides and test banks. Some have noted that while publishers have been around for quite some time in the academic market, with strong established relations with bookstores and often directly with academic departments—sending free textbook copies to faculty and offering customer support—the OER movement has not been able to equal these resources (Ishmael, 2018).

Some of these publisher-generated approaches might be rather inviting for institutions that are breaking into the online education marketplace who have not built out their online courses or who might be operating on a tight timeline and limited budget to invest in online course development. However, those institutions that have a more mature online development structure in place might find this approach too limiting and not sufficiently inclusive of faculty.

Accessibility and ADA Compliance

It is essential for institutions to consider accessibility seriously when adopting or authoring OER, just as it is for online courses in general. Many faculty teaching online might already be familiar with accessibility requirements and regulations and might have an advantage over colleagues who adopt OER but who might be new to online learning. These issues related to accessibility of OER are no different than those for accessibility of other online learning materials.

Most of us working in higher education, whether in a faculty or a support role, are not accessibility experts, unless this is a part of our primary work responsibilities. Some of us might already have gone above and beyond basic familiarity with accessibility issues, since we are using digital learning materials more and more to support even in-person instruction. To ensure that your OER meet accessibility standards, you might want to invest some time and become more familiar with the issues and/or seek support from someone on your campus who can advise and consult with you. See Chapter 4 for more details on OER and accessibility.

Technical Issues

The ubiquitous use of digital learning materials in online education, the use of educational technology to support face-to-face instruction, and competency with educational technology among faculty have been instrumental to the OER movement. A faculty member does not have to have technical expertise to put in an order for a textbook through a bookstore. But when it comes to using OER or other zero-cost materials, instructors need to be willing to develop a facility with digital resources. It does require openness on the part of the instructor to experiment with online resources, learning how to work with OER, and how to troubleshoot or seek assistance for themselves or their students when needed. Because of the digital nature of OER, resources might change or even disappear, and so it is necessary to double-check that these online resources are still available every semester (unless the materials have been downloaded and not just linked to). Depending on the institutional resources, this kind of assistance might be available via teaching assistants, technology fellows, college assistants, or other offices that offer faculty and student support services.

When it comes to addressing technical issues related to OER such as hosting, sharing, and updating—yet again, online educators are more likely to already have a skillset to address most issues. In this way, online educators are a natural resource for promoting best practices with OER at an institution. If an institution is using an OER platform that is linked to a learning management platform, or is a stand-alone, faculty and staff will all need to develop competency in using that platform. As discussed in Chapter 3, learning about institutionally supported OER platforms is essential to ensure success for OER initiatives.

While there are many options to explore among OER hosting providers in order to scale up, it is crucial for an institution to support the chosen OER platform and provide assistance to faculty and students as they adopt and use it. When faculty choose an OER hosting platform that is not institutionally supported, it poses challenges when an institution is attempting to scale up their use of OER. Therefore, institutional leadership needs to be involved and ensure that the OER platform and its support meet faculty and student needs.

OER is still in its infancy. There is a great need for high-quality OER content in every academic subject. But content alone is not enough—when OER is seamlessly integrated as part of a purposeful course design, it can contribute to a high-quality teaching and learning experience. Phylise Banner, Learning Experience Designer and Consultant, shared her vision for OER and the continuing importance of intentional course design:

> *I believe that the OER movement plays a key role in shaping a future where everyone has equitable access to teaching and learning resources. In that future, we will adopt, adapt, create, publish, and share with each other without incurring the high cost of textbooks or other teaching and learning resources. In that future, we will still need to design appropriate learning experiences for our students, and align our courses with the goals and objectives of academic programs and institutions. Design will always matter!*

You, the reader, have an opportunity to contribute to the field of OER. Whether it is writing something for your subject that would not otherwise exist, supporting faculty in their efforts to design and teach their courses with OER, or providing leadership for your institutions to stay at the forefront of the OER movement, your contribution can serve to advance teaching and learning and create more opportunities for all students to succeed.

References

Ishmael, K. (2018, July 10). Rethinking teaching and learning with OER. *New America*. Retrieved from www.newamerica.org/public-interest-technology/blog/rethinking-teaching-and-learning-oer/

Seaman, J. E., & Seaman, J. (2018). *Freeing the textbook: Open education resources in U.S. higher education*. Babson Survey Research Group. Retrieved from www.onlinelearningsurvey.com/reports/freeingthetextbook2018.pdf

Index

CPSIA information can be obtained
at www.ICGtesting.com
Printed in the USA
LVHW022329190423
744855LV00024B/481